# September 11, 2001

DATE DUE

# September 11, 2001

## Attack on New York City

. . .

**WILBORN HAMPTON**

CANDLEWICK PRESS
CAMBRIDGE, MASSACHUSETTS

A Dedication in Love and an Apology
for
Jerel Hampton
Age 1 year, 4 months, 17 days on September 11, 2001

The world you will inherit in a few short years is now rife with hatred.
My generation must accept a certain responsibility for this. We did not pay enough
heed to a divide that opened between the needy and the complacent; we did not
listen with enough attention to the cries of frustration and despair from the other
side. That divide opened into a chasm of enmity that led to the terrible events that
occurred on September 11. It will be the task of your generation to begin building a
bridge across this gulf of hatred. Hatred is born of fear. Do not be afraid.

W. H.

Copyright © 2003 by Wilborn Hampton

Map illustration by Chris Costello

Photo research by Corinne Gill and Lisa Von Seggern

First paperback edition 2007

The Library of Congress has cataloged the hardcover edition as follows:

Hampton, Wilborn.
September 11, 2001 : attack on New York City / Wilborn Hampton. —1st ed.
p.   cm.
Summary: Describes the September 11 attacks in the United States and presents several
personal stories of New Yorkers who lived through the collapse of the World Trade Center.
ISBN 978-0-7636-1949-7 (hardcover)
1. September 11 Terrorist Attacks, 2001—Juvenile literature. 2. Terrorism—United States—
Juvenile literature. 3. Terrorism—New York (State) — New York—Juvenile literature.
[1. September 11 Terrorist Attacks, 2001. 2. Terrorism.]   I. Title.
HV6432.7. H36 2003
974.7'1044—dc21     2002041204

ISBN 978-0-7636-3635-7 (paperback)

2 4 6 8 10 9 7 5 3 1

Printed in the United States of America

This book was typeset in Bembo.

Candlewick Press
2067 Massachusetts Avenue
Cambridge, Massachusetts 02140

visit us at www.candlewick.com

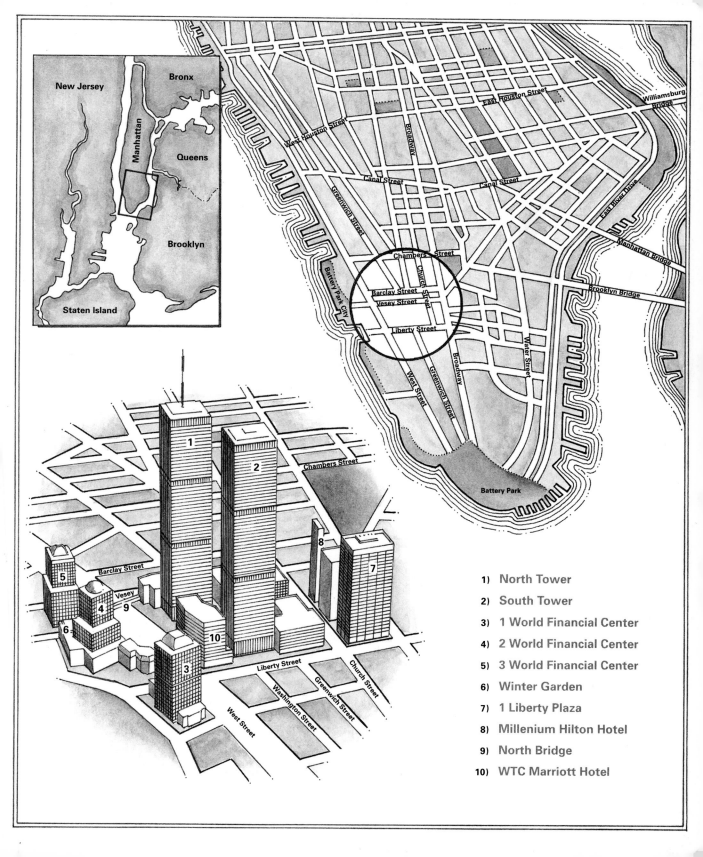

New Jersey

Bronx

Manhattan

Queens

Brooklyn

Staten Island

West Houston Street

East Houston Street

Williamsburg Bridge

Canal Street

Canal Street

Broadway

Greenwich Street

East River Drive

Manhattan Bridge

Chambers Street

Battery Park City

Barclay Street

Church Street

Vesey Street

Brooklyn Bridge

Liberty Street

Broadway

West Street

Greenwich Street

Water Street

Battery Park

Chambers Street

Barclay Street

Vesey

Liberty Street

Church Street

Greenwich Street

Washington Street

West Street

1) **North Tower**

2) **South Tower**

3) **1 World Financial Center**

4) **2 World Financial Center**

5) **3 World Financial Center**

6) **Winter Garden**

7) **1 Liberty Plaza**

8) **Millenium Hilton Hotel**

9) **North Bridge**

10) **WTC Marriott Hotel**

. . . . .

The morning of September 11, 2001, dawned bright and clear in New York City. There had been a steady, soggy rain the night before, but the sunrise that Tuesday brought a brilliant blue sky without a cloud in sight. It was the sort of late summer day that makes you think of baseball more than football, of picnics more than hayrides, of ice cream more than apple pie. It was a day that made you glad just to be alive.

. . . . . . . . . . . . . . . . . . . . .

Then, shortly before 9:00 A.M., just as most New Yorkers were beginning their working day, the city was suddenly and deliberately attacked by hijackers who seized control of two jetliners bound from Boston to Los Angeles and flew them on kamikaze missions into the twin 110-story towers of the World Trade Center. At 8:46 A.M., American Airlines Flight 11, a Boeing 767, flew into the North Tower. At 9:06 A.M., United Airlines Flight 175, another Boeing 767, flew into the South Tower. The planes exploded in fireballs that sent clouds of smoke pouring from the skyscrapers.

In the space of those few minutes, the comfortable world most Americans thought they lived in changed forever. But the horrors of the day were only beginning.

At 9:40 A.M., a third hijacked plane, American Airlines Flight 77, a Boeing 757 en

. . . . . . . . . . . . . . . . . . .

route from Washington, D.C., to Los Angeles, crashed into the Pentagon, the headquarters of America's defense department.

Then, only minutes later, the thing many people had feared, but had tried not to think about, happened. The South Tower, the one into which the second plane crashed, began to collapse. It came down like a tower of dominoes when someone removes one domino from the middle.

Concern immediately grew for its twin, the building that had been hit first. Less than half an hour later, the North Tower tumbled to earth in a mountain of molten rubble. Fires from the 10,000 gallons of fuel that each plane carried raged up to 2,000 degrees, softening the steel girders. The two buildings simply imploded. Steel, concrete, and glass rained from 110 stories in the sky onto city streets jammed with

. . . . . . . . . . . . . . . . . . . .

thousands of frightened people, turning lower Manhattan into a black inferno.

In the time between the collapse of the two towers, a plane crashed in an open field in Pennsylvania, about eighty miles southeast of Pittsburgh. That plane, United Airlines Flight 93, another Boeing 757, had also been seized by hijackers, and authorities assumed that they had intended to fly it into another prominent target, possibly the White House or the Capitol.

In the space of just over an hour, the United States suffered the worst attack in its history. Of four commandeered planes, three had been turned into flying missiles with hundreds of passengers on board. Two had been flown into two giant skyscrapers where thousands of people were quietly at work, and the third had been flown into the home of the nation's defense. And while America grieved at the loss in all four

. . . . . . . . . . . . . . . . . . . .

. . . . . . . . . . . . . . . . . . . .

crashes, it was the first attacks on the World Trade Center and the collapse of the Twin Towers that came to symbolize the collective agony of the day. For those of us who lived in New York, the blow was staggering. Within an hour, the ruins were being called Ground Zero.

Nearly 3,000 people were killed at the World Trade Center, and more than 3,200 children lost a parent. But numbers can't tell the story. The story of what happened in New York that day is told in the accounts of several people who lived through it. Each endured a personal nightmare that day. Each carries different memories. One thing they all remember is how quiet the city was.

. . . . . . . . . . . . . . . . . . .

# THE ATTACK

**JIM KENWORTHY**

■ ■ ■

It was such a glorious day Jim Kenworthy decided to walk to work. Although both Jim and his wife, Ginger Ormiston, had jobs in the complex of buildings that made up the World Trade Center in lower Manhattan, they rarely went to work together. Their two children, Beth and Billie, went to different schools in different parts of the city, and mornings sometimes resembled a fire drill as the four of them scrambled to shower, eat breakfast, dress, and get off to school or work.

As usual, Jim was the first one up that Tuesday. He headed into the kitchen to start the coffee, then went to wake the kids. Billie, who was ten, was the hardest to rouse. But he had to get ready first since he had an early school bus to catch. Billie was just starting the fifth grade at P.S. 6 on the Upper East Side. A school bus stopped at University Place, near Jim and Ginger's apartment off Union Square, but Billie had to be there by 7:30 to catch it. He had missed the bus the previous day and Ginger had to take him to school on the subway, which in turn had made her late for work at her new job as a computer expert with Marsh & McLennan.

After getting the children up, Jim went back to the kitchen to start making breakfast for Beth and Billie. He heard the shower running and knew that Ginger was up. Once the kids were fed, Jim started his own shower while Ginger dressed. He was just getting out when he heard Ginger shout something to him and the front door close. He didn't hear what she said, and he called out to her from the bathroom. But she was gone.

Jim had first met Ginger seventeen years earlier at the wedding of a mutual friend in Pittsburgh. No sparks flew immediately, but when they met again at another wedding two years later, Jim asked Ginger for a date. When they started going out, Ginger and Jim did not seem to have a lot in common. Jim, who was born in Baltimore but grew up in Florida, was working for a small law firm. He loved New York. Ginger, who had an electrical engineering degree from Rutgers and was taking night courses at New York University, still lived with her parents in New Jersey while working at Bell Labs. She was not all that fond of the city. Jim liked baseball and had season tickets to the Yankees, but Ginger did not care much for the game; Jim liked the ballet, while Ginger preferred the opera. But there were many things they both enjoyed. They both loved to try the food of different countries, for example, a pleasure that New York, with its many restaurants, offered. Two years later, Jim and Ginger were married.

They moved into Jim's little one-bedroom bachelor apartment on 17th Street in Manhattan, but after Beth and Billie were born, it became clear they would have to find a bigger place to live. First, they looked for a house in the suburbs, but in the end it was Ginger who decided she did not want to leave Manhattan. The girl from the Jersey suburbs had become a dyed-in-the-wool New Yorker. Eventually, they found a loft near Union Square in downtown Manhattan. It was more than they could afford, and it needed a lot of work. But it became their dream house.

After Billie was born, Ginger stopped working for a while. But when they bought the loft, she knew she would have to find a job again. She started with a big corporation, but after a time she felt she wanted more of a challenge, and over the past year Ginger had changed jobs three or four times, signing on with different start-up Internet companies that always began with great fun, fanfare, and promise but then fizzled as the enterprises ran out of money. She was hoping her new job at M & M, as the giant insurance company was known, would become permanent.

After Ginger left with Billie that morning, Jim and Beth finished dressing and started out toward Beth's school. Beth, who was twelve, was in the eighth grade at New York City Lab School, which was only four blocks away, on 17th Street in Chelsea. Beth was still talking about her soccer match the previous Sunday. Soccer had become a big part of the Kenworthys' lives, and both Beth and Billie played soccer for neighborhood teams, Beth for both a girls' and a boys' team. After dropping Beth off at her school, Jim strolled over to Seventh Avenue and turned south. There is a subway stop at 18th Street and Seventh Avenue, and the train would take Jim directly to the World Trade Center and his job with Deloitte & Touche, an accounting firm. But it was such a beautiful day, he decided to walk the forty-odd blocks to work.

He had just reached the corner of Canal Street when, from somewhere behind and above him, Jim heard a loud noise. He turned around and looked up. It was an airplane flying perilously low over the city. In fact, the big jetliner was so low that it stopped him in his tracks, and he stood watching it from the sidewalk as it streaked south.

The plane listed slightly, then righted itself and, as Jim watched, flew straight into the side of the North Tower of the World Trade Center. Fire and smoke shot out of the building. Jim immediately began counting down the floors from the top of the 110-story skyscraper to where the plane had disappeared into the building. He counted 14. The 96th floor, the same floor where Ginger worked.

**Smoke poured from the North Tower minutes after the attack.**

**BOB FOX**

■ ■ ■

Bob Fox loved being on the water, and whenever he could, he took the ferry across the Hudson River to his job at the World Trade Center. He caught a train from his home in Glen Rock, New Jersey, to Hoboken, then took either the PATH subway or the boat to Manhattan and his office on the 39th floor of the North Tower of the Trade Center. On September 11, Bob took the ferry.

Bob was the director of the Cultural Institutions Retirement System, a company that administered a common pension plan for all the employees of the museums and other cultural groups of New York City. He had to be at work early that morning to prepare for a quarterly meeting of the board of trustees that was scheduled to begin at 9:30.

After leaving the ferry, he walked through the Winter Garden, a large glassed-in atrium on the ground floor of the

World Financial Center, which was located between the Trade Center and the river. He saw his old friend Tim O'Sullivan sitting at one of the tables, reading a newspaper and drinking a cup of coffee. Bob stopped to say hello. Tim had been a deputy director at the Bronx Zoo and had served on the retirement system's board until his own retirement four years ago. Athough he now lived in Pennsylvania, he still came into New York for the board's quarterly meetings. Bob chatted briefly with Tim. They both agreed it would be a perfect day to be playing golf. Bob told Tim he would see him later, then walked across to the Trade Center and took the elevator to his office.

Bob first met Tim soon after he went to work at the New York Botanical Garden, his first real job after college. Bob was born in Washington, D.C., and grew up in nearby Arlington, Virginia. When it came time to go to college, he chose Fordham in New York City, mainly because it had a good rowing team. By the time he graduated with a degree in economics in 1973, the country was still involved in the Vietnam War. Bob figured he would be drafted into the army, so he took a series of short-term jobs—working in a car wash in New Jersey and driving a cab in New York.

He also began dating Tony Fizzuoglio, a girl he had met at Fordham. He was living with several other guys in the

Bronx, and Tony was living in Brooklyn and studying art at the Pratt Institute. When Bob's number failed to come up in the draft lottery, both his search for employment and his subway romance took a more serious turn. The job hunt landed him at the Botanical Garden, and he married Tony. After the birth of their two sons, Michael and Guy, they moved to New Jersey.

Bob and Tim O'Sullivan came into frequent contact in their respective jobs with the New York Botanical Garden and the New York Zoo, which share 500 acres of the heart of the borough in what is known as Bronx Park. Not only were the Zoo and the Garden across the street from each other, they also shared some basic interests. As Bob liked to explain it, the Zoo produced manure and the Garden needed fertilizer.

Bob took to Tim immediately. Tim was an imposing Irishman who stood six feet seven and weighed 270 pounds. He was a great storyteller, and he liked to act out all the parts, complete with accents, whether Irish, Italian, French, or Bronx. People who met Tim never forgot him. He had grown up in the Bronx, and he loved New York. Not only did he have the Irish gift of gab, he was an avid reader, especially of military history, and he could hold his own in a conversation on just about any topic under the sun.

Bob and Tim became especially close during New York City's fiscal crisis in the mid-1970s. The city was cutting jobs right and left, and Bob and Tim both had to be creative to keep jobs at their respective institutions. When Tim heard of an opening in the Cultural Institutions Retirement System, he recommended Bob for the job.

Shortly before 9:00 A.M. that Tuesday, Bob, Tim, and Ray Miller, one of Bob's assistants, were together in Bob's office, waiting for the board meeting. Since his retirement, Tim had faced a series of health problems. He had undergone bypass heart surgery, and he had since had a pacemaker implanted. He suffered from various ailments, and today his hip was hurting.

A delivery boy had just brought up some muffins to go with the coffee at the board meeting, and Bob had gotten up to give him a tip. It was then he heard it. Beginning faintly, then building in intensity, came the sound of a long, low, whirring whine, ending in a scream. Then the building began to sway.

Bob's office had a window on the north side of the tower, and he rushed over to look out of it. Glass, concrete, and bits of steel were falling like rain outside. Someone in an outer office had a radio on. The report was that an airplane had hit the Trade Center.

**OMAR RIVERA**

■ ■ ■

Every working day, Omar Rivera and Salty, his yellow Labrador dog, made the thirty-five minute train ride from the suburb of New Rochelle, New York, to Grand Central Terminal in New York City, then took a subway to downtown Manhattan and Omar's job at the Port Authority of New York and New Jersey, the agency that ran all the ports and airports in both states and that had its headquarters in the World Trade Center.

In cold or wet weather, Omar and Salty would catch the shuttle train to Times Square on the west side of Manhattan and take the Number 1 subway, which had a stop directly under the World Trade Center. But on pleasant days, Omar would take the Number 6 subway downtown from Grand Central and walk across lower Manhattan to the Twin Towers. As he explained it, he liked to "see" the different parts of the city.

What he meant was that he loved to hear the birds and smell the trees and listen to the sounds of the city. For the past fifteen years, Omar had been blind.

Omar loved New York. Born and raised in Colombia, he first came to the city as a college student, when he still had his sight. He went everywhere, walking the streets, going to museums, and looking at the skyscrapers. Years later, after he had become blind, Omar often amazed people by describing pictures he had seen in museums and the architectural detail on certain buildings.

Omar returned to Colombia and finished his degree in engineering. He also married Sonia, his high school sweetheart, and their first two daughters—Elizeth and Andrea Catalina— were born. Omar was working on a hydroelectric project on a river in the Colombian jungle, his first job as a civil engineer, when his eyes began to fail. He had been born with myopia, and when he was fifteen, he had surgery to try to correct his vision. But a small cut on his cornea during the operation had left scar tissue. The scarring had created an obstruction in his eye, which led to glaucoma.

Omar decided to return to the United States to try to find help from a specialist to save his sight. He went from doctor to doctor, but in the end, there was nothing they could do. Within eight months he was totally blind.

Omar realized he would have to give up his career in engineering and learn a new profession. He and Sonia decided to stay in New York because Omar would have better opportunities there to build his new life. Among the challenges they faced was the fact that Omar spoke little English, and Sonia none. But he bought records and tapes and a radio and was fluent within six months. It was also during this time that their third daughter, Erica, was born.

On his first visit to New York, Omar had seen a technology exhibition in which a computer was attached to a synthesizer and could be operated by voice commands. He discovered a training program run by IBM and Baruch College, and while Sonia took odd jobs to help support them, Omar spent the next year in a crash course in learning to operate a computer. There were morning and afternoon classes, all day, every day. Half the students dropped out. But at the end of a year, Omar had a new profession as a computer expert.

Perhaps the biggest task Omar had to face was learning how to walk again. Shortly after he lost his sight, Omar had started lessons in walking with a cane. But he had little success. His body stayed rigid as he tapped down the street, feeling his way along. He felt as though he had no freedom of movement. It was taking him too long to move from one place to another.

After two months of lessons, Omar had managed to go only about two blocks on his own.

One day, his instructor asked Omar if he liked dogs. Omar said he had always loved dogs. His instructor put him in a car and drove him to Yorktown, Long Island.

Their destination was an organization called Guiding Eyes for the Blind, which is run by Bill Badger. Omar moved to Badger's house and began yet another course of intense training. For the next six weeks, Omar and a black Labrador retriever named Ryder lived together and got to know each other. Man and dog learned each other's every move. For Omar, walking down the street with the dog was the closest feeling to freedom he had experienced since he lost his sight. By the end of the training course, Omar had learned to trust the dog with his life. But after five years, Ryder had a heart attack and died. Salty, a yellow Lab, is Omar's third dog. Omar and Salty became inseparable.

September 11 was such a beautiful day, Omar and Salty took the Number 6 subway downtown from Grand Central and walked across lower Manhattan to the Trade Center. In the plaza in front was a fountain. It was a landmark to Omar, and he and Salty often stopped to listen to the gurgling water and the chirping birds that were always splashing around it. But that morning, the fountain was turned off, and he went straight up to his office on the 71st floor of the North Tower.

At about 8:45 A.M., Omar, who was a senior computer systems designer at the Port Authority, finished making some final changes on a presentation he had to give that morning. He gave his computer the command to print out the report. Salty was lying nearby. Omar got up from his desk to collect the papers when he felt a sudden jolt. He knew something had hit the building because he could feel it begin to move back and forth, and the steel girders in the skyscraper were making a loud crackling noise. Omar also heard glass breaking. A lot of glass.

There were not many people in the office at that time of the morning, but somewhere outside his cubicle, several people began to scream. He could sense a whirlwind of paper flying around the office, and when he heard a crash nearby, he knew that his computer had fallen off his desk.

Salty was very nervous. The dog leaped up, then began to run in and out of Omar's cubicle, whining and confused. Omar sat down and began to pray. Just then Salty came in from one of his forays into the main office. He went to Omar and sat right beside him, nudging up against him as close as he could get. It was Salty's way of telling Omar they had to leave. Omar put the dog's harness on him, then stepped out into a chaos he could not see but that he knew he had to escape.

When the first plane flew into the North Tower, the skyscraper began to sway and fill with smoke, and the steel girders began to creak.

**LADDER COMPANY 6**

■ ■ ■

The firefighters of Ladder Company 6 were preparing for the nine o'clock morning shift change. Matt Komorowski, who had been on night duty, was standing in front of the firehouse on Canal Street in Chinatown, waiting to go home. Captain Jay Jonas was in the firehouse kitchen, eating a bowl of cereal. The four other men on duty that morning—firefighters Bill Butler, Sal D'Agostino, Tom Falco, and Mike Meldrum—were inside going about their daily routine. Suddenly, Komorowski heard a loud noise. He glanced up and saw an airplane shoot between two buildings. He knew that it was flying too low, that something was wrong.

No sooner did Komorowski turn and head back into the firehouse to report what he had seen than the duty watchman announced over the intercom that an airplane had just hit the World Trade Center.

Within minutes, all five men were in their gear and heading across town. They parked their fire truck on West Street, at the side of the North Tower. As they jumped down from the ladder truck, they looked up to see the top 20 floors of the skyscraper on fire. Debris was raining from above, and they had to run zigzag across the plaza, dodging chunks of the building, just to get inside. Shattered glass already covered the lobby, and ash was swirling around. As they entered the building, they saw a woman running toward them whose hair and clothes had been burned off. She passed them on the way out. Then they saw two bodies on the floor.

Some firefighters from other units were already on the scene, and a makeshift command center had been set up in the lobby to coordinate a plan of action. The chiefs were trying to determine how far down the fire had spread. But communications were broken, and the men were having a difficult time getting exact information.

The chiefs figured that the blaze already had reached the 80th floor. Firefighters would have to go up the stairs to put it out because few elevators were working, and there was a danger that burning jet fuel from the plane might cascade down the elevator shafts. That meant the firefighters would have to climb up 80 flights, each carrying more than 60 pounds of equipment. Even if they averaged a floor a minute, it would

Within minutes a second plane dropped out of the sky and, as thousands
of New Yorkers watched in horror, flew straight toward the South Tower.

be nearly an hour and a half before they could reach the flames and begin fighting the fires.

As the firefighters waited in the lobby for assignments from their captains, a sharp jolt shook the North Tower. No one immediately knew what had happened. Perhaps it was a delayed explosion from the plane that had flown into the building. Then a firefighter ran into the lobby from outside and said a second plane had crashed into the South Tower. "My God," Captain Jonas said to his men, "they're trying to kill us."

The fire chiefs in the lobby of the North Tower made a difficult decision. Both towers had to be evacuated immediately. The first priority was to get all civilians out of the buildings. They would fight the fires later.

Captain Jonas was at the command post, waiting for his orders. Deputy Chief Pete Hayden looked at him and said, "Jay, just go up and do the best you can."

Jonas went back to his men and told them they were going up into the building.

"This is going to be a long climb," he said. "I know it's going to be hard, but that's what we're doing." The men of Ladder Company 6 then moved toward Stairwell B.

**MAYOR GIULIANI**

∎ ∎ ∎

Mayor Rudolph Giuliani was at a private breakfast meeting at a hotel on Fifth Avenue in midtown Manhattan when one of his deputies received a call that a plane had flown into the North Tower of the World Trade Center. Within minutes, the mayor was in a car speeding downtown.

As the mayor's car passed St. Vincent's Hospital in Greenwich Village, he noticed stretchers and doctors and nurses out on the sidewalk. Just then a fireball exploded in the sky ahead of him. The second plane had just flown into the South Tower. Giuliani knew immediately that he was faced with a crisis unlike anything he had ever imagined.

By the time they arrived near the scene, debris from both crashes was falling like a hailstorm, and Giuliani's car had to stop at Barclay Street, two blocks north of the Trade Center.

When Giuliani got out, he saw New York Police Commissioner Bernard Kerik. Kerik had little information. He said the city seemed to be under an air attack and suggested that all airspace around New York City be closed off and that they call in support from the air force. But Kerik didn't know what number to call to do that.

When Giuliani and his party arrived downtown, they discovered that their cellphones were not working, so a top priority was to find working telephones. The mayor had an underground command center with modern communications in building Number 7 of the Trade Center on Vesey Street, directly across the plaza from the North Tower. But by the time they arrived, it was being evacuated. The mayor then walked toward West Street, where the fire department had a temporary command post.

When they turned the corner at West Street, Giuliani stopped and looked up at the giant skyscrapers. It was the first time he had a clear view of the buildings. All he could see was smoke and flames pouring out of the upper floors. Then, as he was gazing up, he saw a man jump from one of the blown-open windows at about the 100th floor of the North Tower. Transfixed, Giuliani watched the man all the way down, then involuntarily put his hand to his mouth and turned his eyes away.

**New Yorkers watched helplessly from the streets below as the Twin Towers burned and workers in the buildings screamed for help.**

At the fire post on West Street, Chief Peter J. Ganci was in charge. He told the mayor that he believed everybody below the fire line could be saved. He did not have to say what that meant for those above it. On the street, Giuliani ran into Father Mychal Judge, a Franciscan priest who was chaplain to the fire department and also a personal friend. He asked Father Judge to pray for them.

The mayor turned back toward Barclay Street, searching for any place with working telephones. At 75 Barclay Street, he found an office building that was open. The mayor and his party rushed in and started picking up phones on desks. One of the first calls the mayor made was to issue an order summoning all firefighters and police officers in New York City to report for duty. They had been in the Barclay Street office only a few minutes when they heard a large rumbling noise, and the front of the building fell into the street. The room filled with dense smoke. The South Tower had just collapsed.

**The South Tower erupted in a fireball, sending glass and debris cascading onto terrified crowds trying to flee lower Manhattan.**

Everybody in the Barclay Street office dove for cover or fell on the floor. They knew they would have to leave, but they could not go out the front of the building because of the debris that was cascading down. A security guard led the mayor and his party to the basement. After trying several locked doors, they finally found one that opened. It led into an underground tunnel and they emerged a block away in the lobby of a building at 100 Church Street.

Then, covered with dust and with a mask in one hand that he periodically lifted to his mouth, Giuliani started walking north, joining the thousands of other New Yorkers fleeing the chaos of the Trade Center. Along the way he saw a couple of television reporters and began holding a walking news conference. As the mayor made his way up the street, he turned to people alongside him and, in the calm and reassuring voice that became a hallmark of his leadership that day, talked to them, urging those that had facemasks to use them and for everyone not to panic and to "keep walking north."

Giuliani himself was walking north on Church Street, about a dozen blocks from the Trade Center, when the North Tower collapsed. Clouds of smoke several stories high rolled out of the streets of lower Manhattan like giant waves in an ocean storm. The mayor started running. Giuliani and his party

**Mayor Giuliani, with a mask in one hand, joined others fleeing the area and talked briefly with reporters.**

ducked briefly into a hotel lobby just below Canal Street but emerged again a few moments later and continued their march north until they reached a firehouse on the corner of Sixth Avenue and Houston Street. Then, for the next hour or so, New York City was run from a firehouse in Greenwich Village.

**MAC LAFOLLETTE**

■ ■ ■

Mac LaFollette had an early meeting in midtown that morning. Mac worked for Fenway Partners, a New York company despite being named for the Boston Red Sox baseball stadium, and he was helping negotiate the sale of a family business that was being contested by some members.

It was a tense meeting, and the family had left instructions that they were not to be disturbed under any circumstances. But shortly before 9:00 A.M., a woman came in and told the head of the family he had an urgent telephone call. She was clearly upset and insisted he take the call. He left for a few moments and returned to say that a plane had just flown into the World Trade Center. The meeting continued.

When the second plane hit the South Tower, the woman came back in and told them what had happened. The meeting then broke up.

Mac found a taxi and headed back to his own office, also in midtown. The streets were already filled with people staring downtown at the fire and plumes of smoke that were rising over the city. Mac noticed that for a Tuesday morning in midtown Manhattan, it was strangely quiet. No horns, no shouting, no hum, no bustle.

When the towers fell, Fenway Partners decided to close. Mac walked across town to his wife Dawn Davis's office, which was also shutting down. Then the two of them walked downtown together to their apartment in the Chelsea section of the city.

Both Mac and Dawn had grown up in California—he in San Francisco, she in Los Angeles—but they had come to love New York. An old friend of Mac's from San Francisco, Andy Cummins, was staying with them. When Mac and Dawn arrived home, Andy had the television on.

For a couple of years after he graduated from Harvard and before returning to the university's business school, Mac had traveled to several third-world countries, places like Namibia, Nicaragua, Cuba, Vietnam, and had written some articles about them. He was a man used to action, and as he and Dawn and Andy watched the unfolding events in downtown Manhattan, a sense of helpless frustration began to take hold of him, and he decided he had to do something to try to help.

**MY STORY**

■ ■ ■

My day began like any other. Coffee and the newspaper. The dining area in our apartment in an old brownstone house in Greenwich Village is situated under a skylight, and it was awash in glorious sunshine that morning. I was sitting at the dining table, reading the paper and sipping a mug of coffee. My wife, LuAnn Walther, had already left for her job as an editor at a publishing house. She had a busy morning ahead of her with a series of meetings scheduled to begin at 9:00 A.M.

The sound was unmistakably that of an airplane. It is not a sound one often hears in Greenwich Village. Occasionally a helicopter might fly over, but this was different. This was loud, a large commercial airliner, and it was clearly flying very low. I put the paper down and looked up through the skylight, but I saw nothing. I sat quite still, listening as I stared up at the sky through the tops of the trees and neighboring buildings. But the noise went away and I heard nothing more. I went back to reading the newspaper.

Several minutes later, the telephone rang. I nearly didn't answer. New York City was having a primary election that day, and we had been getting a flood of automated calls from politicians begging for our vote. They were a major nuisance, and my first thought was to let the answering machine take the call. But then I thought it might be LuAnn needing something for her meetings, so I answered.

"Bill, this is Jennifer," the voice said.

It took me two or three seconds to register that it was my wife's niece calling from California. When I did, my first thought was that something bad had happened there. After all, it was only 6:00 A.M. in California.

"Are you guys okay?" she asked, but it was not in the casual tone with which one usually asks after someone else's welfare. There was a quavery tension in her voice.

"Sure," I replied, a little cautiously, still thinking that something must be wrong in California for her to be calling so early.

"Is LuAnn all right?" she persisted.

"She's fine," I assured her. "She's already gone to work. We're both okay. Why?"

"Oh," she said, realization coming to her. "You don't know what's happened. Two planes have crashed into the World Trade Center. Both towers are on fire."

It was a moment before I took in what Jennifer had just said. I couldn't quite picture in my mind what she was describing. I went over and turned on the television. Seeing it did not make it any easier to believe.

Nothing Hollywood could ever dream up could compare to what was being shown on live television from downtown Manhattan. Both of the Twin Towers were belching fire and smoke. People were fleeing, streaming out of the area. Firefighters were racing into the two buildings. But how do you even begin to put out fires like that, nearly 100 stories up in the sky? I did not even want to think about how many people might be dead.

The news was breaking so fast that even television was having a difficult time keeping up. Another hijacked plane crashed into the Pentagon. Within minutes there were announcements that New York City's airports were being shut down, then that all bridges and tunnels leading to Manhattan were being closed. The primary elections were called off. Then it was announced that all flights except for those of military planes were grounded throughout the United States. Planes that were already in the air were ordered to land at the

President Bush was interrupted during a school visit by his chief of staff, Andrew Card, who told him about the second attack on the World Trade Center.

nearest airport. International flights on the way to the United States were diverted to Canada. The entire country seemed to be shutting down.

President Bush appeared briefly on television from Florida, where he had been visiting a school. But he only repeated what everybody else had already seen. A short time later, it was announced that the president was flying to an air force base in Louisiana rather than returning to Washington. There were reports that other planes had been hijacked, including one that had crashed into a field in southwest Pennsylvania, and that the White House or the Capitol was a target for attack.

**Some victims were treated for cuts and burns on the street by emergency service workers and doctors who raced downtown after the attacks.**

All of this grim news was being played against a television backdrop of the blazing Twin Towers and scenes of pandemonium in lower Manhattan. Some of the images were almost too painful to watch. The cameras caught faces at windows of the buildings, people trapped on the floors above where the planes hit, screaming in terror, pleading for help as flames and smoke swirled around them. Helicopters were hovering overhead, but there was no way for them to land on the roof because of the fires. There was one horrible picture of a man who leaped to his death from near the top of one of the buildings. And, we learned later, he was only one among many to take that way out.

After being riveted to the television coverage of this devastation for more than two hours, I suddenly realized I was very late for work. I knew the subways were not running and that I would have to walk to Times Square, where I was employed as an editor at *The New York Times*.

It was hard to believe that what I had been witnessing was taking place just down the street from our apartment. From our back garden, the sky was still clear and blue, and apart from an odd siren, which one might hear on any normal day, the city seemed peaceful and quiet. When I stepped out the front door of our apartment, there was little to indicate it was anything other than a beautiful late summer day.

But when I got to Sixth Avenue, I realized I was in a war zone. The avenue was full of hundreds, maybe thousands, of people, walking down the middle of the street, looking neither left nor right, but heading north with grim determination, as though each had an appointment and was running a little late. Some were wearing masks. Some held handkerchiefs over their mouths. Some had torn or burned clothing hanging off them. Some were bleeding. Then I looked downtown.

The cloudless blue sky was obscured by columns of spiraling black, black, black smoke, billowing straight up. And fires danced all around. I stepped into the middle of the street and joined the crowds.

We looked like old newsreel pictures of refugees fleeing a bombed city during World War II. Or of Bosnia just a few years ago. The only thing missing was that nobody had their belongings piled on a donkey cart or in a wheelbarrow.

There was no traffic on the avenue. Occasionally an ambulance heading south would part the sea of people, but then the avenue would fill up again just as soon as it passed. Many seemed to have no destination in mind. They were just going in the opposite direction of the inferno that was raging downtown. It was oddly quiet. Few people talked. But then there was nothing really to say. There were no words to describe what had just happened.

**MOHAMED ATTA**

■  ■  ■

The morning began quite differently for Mohamed Atta. He and Abdulaziz Alomari woke up at about 5:00 A.M. in a motel in South Portland, Maine. They had driven to Portland just the day before in a car they had rented in Boston, arriving in the late afternoon. They planned to spend the night in Portland, then catch a plane back to Boston early the next morning. Atta, at least, knew that it would be the last morning of his life.

Mohamed Atta was born in Cairo, the third child and only son of an Egyptian lawyer and a mother who doted on him as the baby of the family. He had been shy as a child, an introvert who rarely played with the other boys. His ambitious and strict father, also named Mohamed, used to complain to his mother that she was spoiling him. He would tell her that she was raising three girls, that he had three daughters. His father used to tell him that he had to stop being a mama's boy. But young Mohamed was as devoted to his mother as she was to him and continued to sit on her lap until he went to college.

Atta was a bright student, and his father kept urging him to study harder. His father wanted him to be an engineer, and Atta dutifully followed his father's bidding. After graduating from Cairo University in 1990, Atta was accepted to Hamburg Technical University in Germany. At the start, Atta was the same young man who had left Cairo—polite, neat, timid, but a loner. His one social outlet was through his religion. Though not strongly devout, the Atta family had been good Muslims, and Mohamed had begun praying when he was thirteen, the age when Muslim boys are expected to begin prayers.

In Germany, Atta attended Al Tauhid mosque, which was located in the back room of a small shop. The imam, Ahmed Emam, was a militant Muslim who preached that America was the chief enemy of Islam. Slowly, friends noticed a change in Atta. He began to adhere closely to Islamic dietary laws, refusing to drink alcohol and asking about the ingredients of dishes at restaurants. He grew a beard and brought a prayer rug to work. During this time Atta also moved into an apartment with some new friends. One of them was Marwan al-Shehhi, an expatriate from the United Arab Emirates.

In late 1997, Atta left Hamburg and stayed away for more than a year. He returned in early 1999, and it is generally assumed that he spent his sabbatical in Afghanistan at a camp operated by Al Qaeda, the militant Islamic organization run by Osama bin Laden.

Atta came to the United States in the summer of 2000. He shaved his beard and traveled to Florida, where he got in touch with his friend from Hamburg, Marwan al-Shehhi. In the fall of that year, Atta received a bank transfer of $100,000 from an unknown source, and both Atta and al-Shehhi signed up to take flying lessons at Huffman Aviation in Venice, Florida. They paid $10,000 each by check.

After arriving in Portland on the evening of September 10, Atta and Alomari checked in at a Comfort Inn on a stretch of highway known as Maine Mall Road. The two men stayed in their room for a couple of hours, then left the motel about 8:00 P.M. and drove to a nearby Pizza Hut. After eating, they stopped by two ATM machines at separate locations, then drove to a gas station, where they filled up their rented silver blue Nissan Altima. Afterward, they drove to Scarborough, a town a few miles south along I-95, and went into a Wal-Mart outlet. They stayed about twenty minutes but bought nothing. They then went back to their motel and did not leave again

**Mohamed Atta, right, and Abdulaziz Alomari were photographed by
a security camera at the Portland airport as they raced to check in
for their flight to Boston with only fifteen minutes to spare.**

until they checked out the following day just after 5:30 A.M.
They had half an hour to catch their flight.

They left their rental car in the parking lot directly across
from the Portland airport entrance. They checked in at the US
Airways counter, went through security, and boarded a flight
to Boston that departed at 6:00 A.M. Less than an hour after
landing at Boston's Logan Airport, they boarded American
Airlines Flight 11, bound for Los Angeles. But by this time

they were not alone. Three other members of the hijacking crew also got on the American Airlines flight in Boston.

As American Flight 11 waited for takeoff that morning, Mohamed Atta, sitting in seat 8D, pulled out his cellphone and dialed a number. The call rang on another cellphone only a few planes behind him in the same line of aircraft waiting to take off. Atta's old friend from Hamburg, Marwan al-Shehhi, who was sitting in seat 6C aboard United Airlines Flight 175, answered. No one knows exactly what was said. The call lasted less than a minute. It is generally assumed it simply confirmed that their terrorist mission, a plan they had spent years preparing, was on.

# FLIGHT

**JIM KENWORTHY**
*"No one talked."*

After watching the huge skyscraper swallow up the plane, Jim Kenworthy instinctively started running toward the building where his wife worked. After one block, he thought of Beth and Billie. He turned and ran in the other direction, toward Beth's school. Jim had run two blocks back north when it occurred to him that Ginger might be lying wounded, unconscious even, somewhere in the World Trade Center. He should be trying to find her. He stopped and turned around again and started running south. After one block, he halted. He had gone four blocks in two directions and was now in exactly the same spot where he had watched the jetliner disappear into the side of the North Tower. He stood dazed, helpless, quite literally not knowing which way to turn.

Jim tried to calm down and think rationally. If Ginger had survived the crash of the jet into her floor of the building, she would try to call him. Jim pulled out his cellphone and started calling any possible number that Ginger might have dialed. He first tried their home number. But the machine said there were no new messages. He then called his office, then her office, then home again, then his sister Barbara in Brooklyn.

Jim finally got through to his sister. He told her what he had seen and where he was and that he was going to need some help. It was while he was standing on the street, talking to his sister in Brooklyn, that Jim heard an explosion from somewhere in the area of the World Trade Center. He looked up but saw only the same enormous clouds of smoke pouring out of the gaping gash in the side of the North Tower. From where he stood, he could not see and did not know immediately that a second plane had just flown into the South Tower.

Jim had no illusions that the plane crash into the North Tower had been an accident. He had watched the jetliner on its approach down Seventh Avenue, and it had made a beeline for the skyscraper. And when the plane listed slightly at one point, whoever was in the pilot's seat had quickly righted it so that it would fly straight into the side of the building. But if Jim was convinced that the crash was intentional, he also thought at first that it was probably some crazy person who had somehow commandeered the plane and crashed it into the tower.

But when his sister, who was now watching television in Brooklyn, told him that a second plane had flown into the South Tower, Jim abandoned the thought that the crash he had seen was the work of a lone nut case. He did not have any idea what was happening, but he knew what he had to do. He had to get out of the downtown area and reach his children. If lower Manhattan was under some kind of attack, Jim had to give up any idea of trying to go inside the Trade Center to search for Ginger. He knew that for the sake of the children he could not take the chance of being killed himself.

Jim made one more call home. There were no messages. He then headed east on Canal Street, half walking, half trotting, through Chinatown until he came to the subway stop at Lafayette Street. Although all subway and bus service had already halted on the West Side of Manhattan, some trains were still running on the East Side.

The subway station was crowded with people, but Jim patiently made his way to the platform and got on the first train going uptown. It was a Number 6 local. The train was packed. At every stop, there were scores of people waiting to get on. But nobody was getting off. The train moved at a snail's pace, stopping frequently between stations and then sitting for what seemed like ages at each station. A subway ride that might normally take fifteen or twenty minutes took Jim nearly an hour.

One thing that struck him was that although the train was as crowded as it was at rush hour, no one talked.

When the train finally arrived at 86th Street, Jim made his way off and walked from Lexington Avenue over to Billie's school on Madison Avenue. He found his son, confused and frightened, and learned that no one at the school had told the students what had happened downtown. Jim told Billie about the crash and that his mother was missing, and the two of them left the school to go find Beth.

After his experience on the subway, Jim decided he would try the bus to get back downtown. Jim and Billie walked a block over to Fifth Avenue and got on a bus going south. But the bus was even slower than the subway. In addition to the mass of people fleeing the downtown area on foot, the streets in midtown were jammed with cars. The bus crawled through the traffic. At around 42nd Street, Jim decided they could walk faster than the bus could take them, and he and Billie got off and headed on foot toward Beth's school, about thirty blocks away.

Jim and Billie were walking against the flow of those who were trying to get out of lower Manhattan, and going south on Fifth Avenue was like trying to ski uphill into an avalanche. After a few blocks, they headed west to Eighth Avenue and then turned south. As they went farther downtown, the crowds

**Dazed and fearful, people fled lower Manhattan through streets filled with rubble from the Twin Towers.**

of people coming toward them grew larger. Many of the people were covered in ash, had torn clothing, or were bleeding. Strangers rushed to give a hand or a shoulder to those who faltered. At several of the storefront groceries, known in New York as "Koreans" because of the predominant nationality of their proprietors, clerks were handing out bottles of water to all who passed.

Once again, despite the vast numbers of people on the street, Jim was struck by the fact that it was eerily quiet. Almost no one was talking. And those who were spoke in low, hushed tones. It was as if everybody were in church.

At one point, Jim overheard a man tell someone, "They're gone. They're both gone." He did not have to ask what was gone. Jim realized that both towers had fallen. He and Billie kept walking south. He had only one purpose at this point. All he wanted to do was get his children home.

When they finally reached Beth's school, it was nearly noon, three hours since the attack. For Beth, it had been the most harrowing three hours of her life. Shortly after the planes had flown into the Twin Towers, the teachers at the school had asked the students whether any of them had parents who worked at the World Trade Center. All the students who raised their hands were taken to a private room, where they were told that there had been an attack on the Trade Center and that the school was trying to contact their parents. They were to remain there until their parents could be reached. The school itself was closing, and the rest of the students were told to go home.

Beth was the only student whose parents both worked at the World Trade Center. One by one, the parents of most of the other children were located, and one by one, they were sent home or fetched by relatives. But after nearly three hours of trying to reach Beth's parents, no one at the school could find either of them.

By the time Jim and Billie reached her school, Beth was in

hysterics. When they walked into the room where she was waiting, she leaped up from her chair, raced across the room, and threw herself into her father's arms, sobbing uncontrollably. As the minutes had turned into hours, Beth had become convinced that no one could reach her parents because they were both dead.

. . . . . . . . . . . . . . . . . . . . . . .

## BOB FOX
**"Suddenly, a lot seemed to be happening."**

Bob Fox's first thought on hearing that a plane had struck the North Tower was that it must have been some sort of light plane. A Piper Cub, something like that. Bob had lived through one attack on the World Trade Center, in 1993, when a powerful car bomb had exploded in one of the underground garages. It had been a devastating attack and had prompted an evacuation from the North Tower.

Immediately, however, he noticed there were some differences between the 1993 bombing and what was happening now. Although the offices were beginning to fill with smoke, just as they had in the car bombing, there seemed to be less smoke than before. Also, the office still had electricity. The lights were on, and so were the computers. And the telephones seemed to be working. In the previous bombing, all the lights had gone out immediately, and the phones had gone dead. Maybe, Bob thought, this wasn't that big a deal.

In fact, it was the telephone that brought news of the reality they faced. Joe LoCicero, a friend and colleague who worked in midtown Manhattan, called to see if Bob was all right. Joe, who had been watching television, told Bob that a large commercial jetliner had flown into the building and that the jet had been hijacked. It appeared to be some sort of deliberate attack.

Bob passed on this news to the others who were sitting in his office, and everybody immediately called their homes to let their families know that they were all right. Ray Miller, Bob's assistant, also had been trying to reach the Port Authority security office to find out what they should do. The Port Authority was in effect the landlord for the World Trade Center, and the agency had its own police force that was responsible for all security in the building. It took Ray several tries, but when he did get through to the security office, he was told that everybody in the building should leave as quickly as possible. Ray then went out into the main hallway to check on the elevators but returned to report that they were not working. Ray said several people were already leaving through the main stairwell. Just then, a Port Authority security official came into the office and told them that they would all have to leave immediately.

Tim was still sitting on the couch. He looked up at Bob and told his friend that he was going to need help. Because of his hip, it was going to be hard for him to get down the stairs. Bob told Tim that he and Ray would help him. The three of them started out.

They stopped briefly in the men's room to wet their handkerchiefs to hold over their mouths because of the smoke. Bob also filled a bottle with water. Then they went into the stairwell. Bob placed Tim's arm around his shoulder, and Ray did the same on the other side. It was clearly very painful for Tim to walk down the stairs, and Bob and Ray had to support him every step of the way.

It was difficult going. But it could have been worse. The lights were on inside the stairwell, so they could see. And although the traffic on the stairs was steady, it was not as crowded as they first thought it might be. A few people rushed down past them, but for the most part, the evacuation was very orderly. They met some firefighters who were coming up the stairs, and the people going down cheered them. It struck Bob that almost no one was talking. Occasionally there would be a shout, but it was always from a firefighter or police officer yelling into a walkie-talkie.

Down and down they went. Slowly, slowly. They stopped to rest every few floors. They started on Floor 39, stopped first on Floor 35, and again on 31. Bob saw a firefighter sitting on the stairs, leaning against the wall with his eyes closed. He was grimacing in pain. His buddy was kneeling beside him talking into a walkie-talkie. Bob overheard the words "cardiac arrest."

It was also while they were resting on Floor 31 that Bob felt a sharp jolt. The whole building shuddered, and the stairs shook. They immediately resumed their slow progress down the stairs. They made it down only a few more floors when Tim said he simply could not go any farther.

Two firefighters in the stairwell offered to help. They suggested putting together a makeshift stretcher for Tim. One of them went into an office and came out with a dolly. They leaned Tim against it and tried wrapping fire hose around him to hold him on it. A Port Authority police officer, Captain Kathy Mazza, was also there. She had an oxygen machine with her, and she gave Tim oxygen while the firefighters tried to strap him onto the dolly with strips of fire hose. Tim joked with her about being Italian.

The stretcher didn't really work. They made it down a couple more floors, but Tim kept rolling off the side of the dolly. He was simply too big and heavy to be held steady on it, and the firefighters couldn't balance him. One suggested they find a chair in an office, or a small desk, and went off to look for one.

It was at about the 21st floor that Bob noticed a marked increase in tension in the firefighters who were helping them with Tim. Suddenly, a lot seemed to be happening. Walkie-talkies were crackling, and Bob noticed that the little alarm lights that firefighters wear to alert them to danger were going off repeatedly. The firefighters told Bob and Ray that they should go ahead, that they, the firefighters, would get Tim down. Bob did not want to go, but the firefighters insisted. They told Bob and Ray to leave the building immediately. They would look after Tim.

Bob was tormented. Tim had been more than a mentor and friend. He had been almost like a second father to Bob. He did not want to leave Tim. The firefighters told him he had no choice. He and Ray had to leave the building. Now. Bob said good-bye to Tim. He looked into Tim's eyes, clapped him on the shoulder, and told him they would see each other at the bottom. Then he and Ray started down. When they got to the

As workers in the towers evacuated the buildings down stairwells,
they met firefighters like Mike Kehoe, who were rushing up.

lobby, Bob was surprised at the amount of debris. In the stairwell, he had not realized how much damage the building had
undergone. Chunks of marble and glass were everywhere.

In the lobby, firefighters directed them away from the
main entrance. Bob went through what had been a plate
glass window and was suddenly outside the building. Another

firefighter told the two men to keep walking, just keep walking. They started moving northwest, toward the corner of West and Vesey Streets. It was even worse outside than it had been inside. A whirlwind of debris filled the air. It was like a snowstorm or a hailstorm, only the snowflakes were pulverized glass and the hailstones were bits of the building. And the smoke was so dense Bob could not see more than a few feet in front of him. He passed some fire trucks. Again he was told, "Keep walking."

**The smoke was so dense and the air so thick with debris that some people in downtown Manhattan became disoriented as they tried to escape.**

At some point, he and Ray became separated in the crowd, but Bob kept heading in the general direction of the river. He had almost reached West Street, when first one fire-fighter, then a chorus of voices shouted, "Run! Run! Run!"

He did not have to be told again. He took off as fast as his legs would carry him.

Suddenly Bob heard a loud boom. He thought it must be some sort of explosion from the fire. He instinctively put his briefcase behind his head, but he didn't stop running. Something hit him hard in the shoulder, but still he kept running. He then felt something hit him in the leg. He stumbled but continued running. He thought that maybe he was about to die and said a silent prayer: "God, please don't let me know."

Then, within seconds, the entire world went black. A cloud of thick smoke enveloped him and he found himself in total darkness.

Bob stopped running. He couldn't see and he couldn't breathe. His shoulder throbbed with pain and his leg hurt. He stood still. He stood there forever, maybe a minute or two, then put out his hand. He touched a fire truck, less than a yard away, but he still couldn't even see it. He was lucky he had not run into it. The wind was whipping from all directions. It was dead quiet.

**The South Tower began to collapse.**

It was several minutes before the clouds began to lift. Out of the darkness, Bob heard some people coughing. Then he heard someone scream. He began to move cautiously in the direction of the noise.

At one corner, a police officer gave some oxygen to Bob. He, in turn, offered the officer his bottle of water. Bob saw a doctor on the street and followed him to a triage center that had been set up in the lobby of a hotel near the Hudson River. There were people on the floor with doctors and nurses working over them. A firefighter was standing up against one wall, sweating profusely and looking confused, his arms hanging limply at his sides. Bob realized the man was having a heart attack. It was the second firefighter Bob had seen suffering a heart attack within half an hour.

A doctor came over to look at Bob but decided his injuries could wait. After a few minutes, they were all told there was a gas leak in the hotel and the lobby was not safe. Everyone had to leave. Bob headed toward the river again, his thoughts bouncing like a pinball between his family and Tim and Ray. Although he and Ray had become separated, Bob knew that Ray had gotten out of the building. He had no idea what had happened to Tim.

As Bob wandered along the riverside, his shoulder and leg continued to throb and he felt nauseous. He kept drinking water.

As the South Tower imploded, an avalanche of steel, concrete, and glass cascaded down on lower Manhattan, sending waves of smoke rolling through the streets.

**Firefighters began examining the still smoldering and burning ruins, searching the adjacent streets for survivors from the collapsed towers.**

He could not drink enough water. He felt like he was breathing cement.

A police officer told him that some ferries were running to New Jersey from the north end of Battery Park City, and even escorted him to the pier at Stuyvesant High School on Chambers Street. Bob got on a ferry that took him straight across the river to Hoboken. On the way, he tried to call Tony, but his cellphone did not work.

When Bob landed in Hoboken, he headed straight for the train terminal to try to find a pay phone. He had no idea how terrible he looked until he noticed the stares and heard the gasps of people in the train station when he walked in. His clothes were torn and covered with ash, burned in places, and his face was as black as a coal miner's.

He walked over to the pay phones and fished in his pocket for some change. He had none. He turned and looked at the people who were staring at him as though as he had just stepped off a spaceship from Mars. Then, almost in unison, a crowd of people rushed toward him, asking what could they do for him. He said he needed some change to call his wife. Everyone started going through pockets and purses, emptying them out, offering him whatever coins they had.

**The entire area around the Twin Towers resembled a war zone, with streets covered in debris and wounded survivors wandering around in a daze.**

As Bob turned to call home, his own cellphone rang. Although he had not been able to call out, someone was calling him. He flipped the phone open in a rush. It was Ray, who was calling to say that he was all right. After they had become separated, Ray had also made his way to the river and had gotten there in time to make the last ferry to Jersey City. He was calling from there now. Ray had no news about Tim but said he had called Tony to tell her they had both made it out safely.

There was a train leaving Hoboken within minutes, and Bob was on it. He took a seat by the window, and as the train pulled out of the station, Bob took his first look back across the water. He was stunned. The Twin Towers weren't there. He could hardly believe it. All the way home on the train, he kept wondering, which way did they fall? To the north? To the east? It never occurred to him that they had simply collapsed on themselves.

When Bob reached the station, Tony took one look at him and immediately drove him to the emergency room at the hospital in nearby Ridgeway, New Jersey. As the doctors dressed the wounds in his shoulder and calf, they surmised that something had shot through his shoulder like a bullet, probably some small piece of the North Tower.

Twisted steel girders and chunks of concrete from the two 110-story towers created a mountain of rubble several stories high. Firefighters, police officers, and emergency service workers, along with their canine partners, were joined by civilian volunteers searching for any signs of survivors.

## OMAR RIVERA
### "The air was thick with smoke."

As Omar Rivera stepped out of his cubicle, clutching his lead to Salty, he still did not know exactly what had happened. But he knew that it was something very bad. Several people were screaming, and Omar could hear the sounds of people scurrying to leave. There were other sounds that were even more ominous. There was a crunch of glass underfoot, and the creaking and cracking noises from the walls were increasing.

The offices were also beginning to fill up with smoke. Omar could smell acrid smoke everywhere. For a moment, he could not identify what was different about this smell, but it was making him nauseous. Then he overheard someone shout that an airplane had hit the building just above them, and he realized that what he was smelling was jet fuel burning. He knew he had to leave.

But Salty did not seem to know which way to go. Omar himself had become disoriented and was not sure of the way to the elevators. Just then, someone touched his elbow.

Donna Enright had hired Omar for his job at the Port Authority, and was now his supervisor. Omar was the first person she thought of after the attack. Donna's office was on the southeast corner of the 71st floor of the North Tower. Omar's was on the northwest. Donna knew the elevators were not working, and she had delayed leaving to come all the way around the building to make sure Omar and Salty could reach the stairs.

Omar took Donna's arm with his right hand and held Salty's lead with his left, and the three of them walked quickly toward the stairwell. Methodically, they began to make their way down, floor by floor, stair by stair, step by step.

Although they had reached the stairwell within several minutes of the attack, it was already crowded with people trying to evacuate the burning skyscraper. The air was thick with smoke and getting thicker, and Omar again became queasy from the acrid, oily smell. Donna, Omar, and Salty stayed close together as they descended.

Workers from other offices were pouring into the stairwell at every floor, but everyone moved at a fairly steady pace. And for the most part, everyone was quiet. There was some talking, but it was almost in whispers and kept at a minimum. Occasionally, someone would sob or let out a wail or even start praying aloud, and that would trigger a sudden burst of noise—screaming, moaning, crying—until the surge of fear had spent itself, and then it would stop as abruptly as it had begun, and everyone would move on in silence. For Omar, the entire trip down was punctuated by alternating periods of silence, then noise, then silence, then noise again, and more silence. And all the way down, Omar kept hearing things that others could not—the creaking of the steel girders that held the giant building upright in the sky and the cracking of the walls.

Since Omar could not see where each landing ended, Donna would tell him when they were about to reach the end of a flight of stairs, and Salty would lead the way and guide him in the direction he should take. And as they passed each floor, Donna would tell him where they were—66, 65, 64. At the start, they were making pretty good time—better than a floor a minute. They simply kept moving down the stairs with the crowd . . . 52, 51, 50, 49. Then at the 44th floor, the stairwell they were in ended. They had to re-enter the building, pass through a corridor, another door, another corridor, and enter another stairwell.

At every floor, more people crowded into the stairs, until the narrow space was as jammed as a subway at rush hour. After several flights, they began to encounter firefighters who were coming up the stairs, which meant all those trying to go down had to squash even closer together to make way for them. The firefighters were asking everybody if they were okay, offering oxygen or help if anyone needed it.

**Workers in the towers made their way down smoke-filled stairwells that became more crowded at every floor.**

As they reached the lower floors, water slowed their progress even more. Broken pipes and sprinkler systems had made the stairs slippery. Soon Omar and Donna and Salty found they were sloshing through water two to three inches deep.

At about the 20th floor there was another huge influx of people, and the traffic on the stairs halted in a kind of gridlock. Three or four times Omar, Donna, and Salty had to stop in their tracks and wait until those ahead of them moved on before they could resume their own descent.

At one point, someone suggested to Omar that he could make better time if he did not have to worry about the dog, and tried to take Salty's leash. But Omar held firmly to the Labrador's harness. Nothing would separate him from Salty. As they got near the bottom, there was more glass and concrete underfoot, and water was everywhere. But if the water on the stairs was a hindrance for Omar and Donna, it was blessing for Salty, washing the pads of his paws of glass and other debris.

It was about an hour after they started down that Omar, Donna, and Salty emerged from the stairwell on the plaza level of the North Tower. Suddenly a cacophony of sound assaulted Omar's ears. Inside the stairwell, he had heard only what was immediately around him. But once outside, he was hit by a discordant symphony of ambulance and fire truck sirens and a babble of voices ranging from firefighters shouting on walkie-talkies to fellow evacuees crying, cursing, and praying.

There was one difficult moment when Salty tried to lead Omar through the plaza, the route they took almost daily. But the firefighters were directing Donna to go down one flight to the concourse to exit the building. For a moment, Omar was in the middle as Salty started off in one direction and Donna pulled on his arm to go in another.

When they finally got outside, Omar's first thought was to find some water for Salty, who was panting heavily. In fact, all three were exhausted and bedraggled and thirsty. Donna saw someone handing out free bottles of water on Church Street, and they headed there. As they walked across the plaza, Omar felt something in the air striking his face. It felt like he was walking in a snowstorm. But what was pelting Omar in the face was a swirl of ash and pulverized glass and cement.

As they stopped for water on Church Street, they met a couple of other workers from their office. Omar asked Donna what was happening to the building, what it looked like. Donna turned and looked back at the towers and started to describe what she saw to Omar—the smoke and fires, pieces of the skyscrapers falling.

Suddenly, the South Tower started to collapse with a roar that sounded like a hundred jet planes revving to take off. Donna screamed. They dropped their water and started to run. Everybody ran. Omar clutched Salty's harness and trusted the dog's sense of direction. There were fire trucks, ambulances, police cars, a maze of equipment jammed into the streets along with hundreds of people, all of them running for their lives. But Salty loped through them all, dodging people and machinery, keeping a pace he knew Omar could follow.

They ran and ran until they were exhausted, and then they walked. At 14th Street, Omar and Donna parted. She lived in New Jersey and turned west toward the river. Omar kept going north. His only thought was to get home to his Sonia and his daughters.

Omar and Salty walked all the way to Grand Central Terminal on 42nd Street. When they arrived, it was packed. This in itself was not unusual. But on September 11, thousands of people were crammed elbow to elbow inside the sprawling rail station, and more were waiting outside trying to get in.

The jam was caused by the fact that no trains were running in or out of the city. But Omar was desperate to get home. Like Bob, he had not been able to call home since the attack, and he knew his wife would be frantic with worry.

Omar figured that the trains would start running again at some point, and he wanted to be on one of them. So he and Salty began making their way into the terminal. They inched forward, foot by foot, into the crowd, which was oddly quiet, Salty nosing ahead of Omar, who clung tightly to the dog's lead. Because of his blindness, Omar was used to relying on the kindness of strangers, and strangers did not fail him that day. As Omar and Salty edged into the crowd, people moved aside to let them pass.

Shortly after 1:00 P.M., the authorities decided to open three lines leading out of Grand Central and send one train out on each. One of the trains was on the line that went to New Rochelle, and although there was a crush of people trying to get on it, Omar and Salty made it. They were lucky. Grand Central closed again after those three trains left.

When he arrived at the New Rochelle station, Omar called Sonia. She had been watching television all day with several neighbors who had come by the Riveras' house to be with her in case there was bad news. Some, anticipating the worst, had even brought food. When Sonia heard Omar's voice on the telephone, she shrieked with joy. She had believed he was dead.

## LADDER COMPANY 6
### "First came the noise."

As the men of Ladder Company 6 climbed the stairs in the North Tower, they were cheered by the crowds of people making their way down. Some of the people coming down had been burned, but the evacuation was proceeding calmly. It was almost like a fire drill in school. The firefighters stayed on their right as they ascended the stairs, and the civilians leaving the building stayed on their right as they descended.

Captain Jonas ordered the men to take a break every 8 or 10 floors. He didn't want them to be too tired to do their jobs once they got to the top. They had just reached the 27th floor when the entire building shook like it was in an earthquake. At first no one knew what had happened. All they heard was a roaring whoosh that went on for maybe twenty seconds. When the noise stopped, Jonas went onto one of the floors to look out the windows. He could hardly believe what he saw. The entire South Tower had collapsed. When he returned, he had to give an order to his men that was one of the most difficult he'd ever had to give. Firefighters are not trained to leave a burning building with people still inside it. But Jonas knew that if the South Tower could come down, the North Tower could as well. He told his men to evacuate.

As they made their way down, the firefighters stopped to help people who were still descending from the upper floors. At about the 20th floor, they encountered a woman in her late fifties named Josephine Harris, an employee at the Port Authority who had come down from the 73rd floor. When the men of Ladder 6 met her, she was exhausted. She was a heavy-set woman, and she was clearly having trouble walking down the stairwell. Her legs were swollen and she was moving very slowly.

Billy Butler and Tommy Falco put her arms around their necks and began to help her down the stairs. But she could take only a few steps at a time. Captain Jonas and the other firefighters were eager to get out of the building. But Josephine was slowing them down. Butler kept telling Josephine she had to move faster. But her legs simply would not obey. As they neared the fourth floor, she crumpled to the ground. She began to cry and told them she couldn't walk anymore. She told the firefighters to leave her.

Butler began to talk to her. He asked Josephine about her family. She said she lived in Brooklyn, that she had grown children, and that she was a grandmother. Butler told her to keep trying, that her grandkids would want to see her again, that she had to get home to them. She had to get out for their sakes. The firefighters got her on her feet.

Just then it happened. It was Komorowski who felt it first. He was the last of the six firemen in line, and as a blast of air slammed into his back, he shouted for everyone to start moving. Then it hit full force. First came the noise, a deafening roar that sounded like a jet engine in a subway tunnel. Then came a hailstorm of flying concrete and glass and a cloud of dense smoke and dust that made it almost impossible to breathe. The North Tower was collapsing around them.

The firefighters were hurtled downward in a virtual free fall with slabs of concrete, pieces of glass, and steel beams flying past them. The noise was louder than anything they had ever heard before, and the rush of wind tossed them about like a tornado. Komorowski was thrown over the heads of the firefighters in front of him and ended up two floors below them. Captain Jonas curled up into the fetal position on the stairwell landing. He thought he was going to die for certain. The building shook so violently that it bounced him up and down like a basketball.

The men could hear nothing except what sounded like a series of explosions that went on interminably in rapid succession, *boom, boom, boom, boom, boom,* and the screeching sound

**Clouds of smoke from the collapse of the North Tower engulfed lower Manhattan.**

of steel beams and girders that were being twisted like plastic ties on a loaf of bread. Even when the noise stopped and dead silence fell on the stairway, a deluge of concrete and metal continued to pelt the firefighters. Three of them had their helmets knocked off. When it was over, they were all surprised to find they were still alive.

Captain Jonas did a roll call, and each of the firefighters of Ladder 6 answered. Then some other voices came out of the darkness in the stairwell between the second and fourth floors. Among them were two other firefighters, a Port Authority police officer, and a fire battalion chief, Richard Picciotto, an old friend of Captain Jonas, who had also been helping civilian stragglers out of the building. Then, covered with ash and rising out of the debris like a ghost coming out of a grave, Josephine Harris sat up.

At first the firefighters did not know how much of the North Tower had fallen. It was smoky and pitch dark, and the only lights came from their flashlights. Captain Jonas thought that perhaps they could dig their way out to the building's lobby. Chief Picciotto and Komorowski, who were together two floors below Jonas and the others, pried open a door on the second-floor landing. But all they found was compacted rubble.

As the firefighters surveyed their situation, there were some positives. They all had their pickaxes and hooks and ropes.

They noticed a fire sprinkler pipe intact, so they would have water. They could also see what remained of an elevator shaft, and Jonas considered trying to lower themselves down by ropes. But if they got to the bottom and found it blocked, as the second-floor entry had been, they would not be able to climb back up again. It was a possible way out, but one he decided to try only as a last resort.

Almost from the time they landed, the firefighters started sending out calls for help on their radios, but no one was responding. Captain Jonas told the others to turn off their lights and radios. He had begun to worry that they might be trapped for days, and he wanted to conserve batteries. Only he and Chief Picciotto would try to reach the outside world on their radios, and for the next hour they sent out "Mayday" calls into the void.

As the men and Josephine waited, sending out calls for help and hearing only silence in return, the awful prospect came to each of them that they might have survived the collapse of the tower only to die in the tomb where they had fallen. The firefighters took turns talking to Josephine, trying to cheer her up, holding her hand and telling her that everything would be all right, that help was on the way, even though as far as they knew, no one was aware they were alive.

Finally, Captain Jonas heard a voice at the other end of his radio. It was from a deputy fire chief who asked for Jonas's location. When Jonas told him they were all in Stairwell B in the North Tower, the fire chief asked, "Where is the North Tower?" From outside, all the firefighters on the street could see was a sea of rubble. They had no way of knowing where Stairwell B or even the North Tower had been. It was the first hint to the men of Ladder 6 that the entire building had collapsed.

The trapped firefighters and Josephine waited and waited for a rescue party to reach them. Chief Picciotto also reached a firefighter on the outside, and was told that rescuers were on the way. But still no one came.

Then, after two more hours of waiting and with their hopes for a rescue beginning to fade, Picciotto looked up in the smoky darkness and thought he saw a pinprick of light. For a moment he thought he was hallucinating. The light appeared then went away. Then it appeared again. He called up to Jonas to ask if he saw it, too. Then they all saw it and watched as it grew bigger and bigger, first the size of a baseball, then a basketball. They had been trapped in total darkness for about three and a half hours, and it was only now that the smoke from the collapse and the fires in adjacent buildings had cleared enough to let the sunlight creep through.

Picciotto decided to try to reach the opening. With Josephine and the other firefighters watching him, he scrambled up toward the light, getting a toehold here and stepping on a wedge of concrete there. Once he got to it, he realized that the hole looked out onto a sort of balcony on the stairs that was still several stories above ground. But he also saw open sky. One by one, Meldrum, D'Agostino, Falco, and Komorowski climbed up to join him while Jonas and Butler stayed behind with Josephine.

As they gazed on the moonscape of destruction around them, they also saw a firefighter's helmet bobbing along the rubble, moving toward them about 100 feet away. The rescue party from Ladder 43 was finally arriving. Captain Jonas and Butler joined the others on the ledge, and the firefighters decided it would be easier for them to climb down to the ground from the balcony than for the rescuers to climb up to where they were.

The way down was an almost sheer drop, like that of a rock face, only instead of crags and broken stone, the outcroppings were of hot jagged metal and steel beams. Picciotto wanted to go first. Captain Jonas and Butler, both of whom were rope experts and taught rescue courses, rigged up a complicated rope operation involving what is known as a Munter hitch, which works like a seat belt. With that knot, the men would be able to pull Picciotto back up if he fell. By the time they were finished, Picciotto had a loop of rope around his legs and chest, making a sort of harness. He started out.

In effect, Picciotto rappelled down the side of the North Tower ruins. But rather than swing out and back as a rock climber might, he inched his way down, metal beam to steel girder, like climbing down from the top of a tree, branch by branch.

As the men of Ladder 6 followed in Picciotto's footsteps, making their way down to the ground, the rescuers of Ladder 43 started climbing up. The first to arrive was Lieutenant Glenn Rohan, who immediately went into the stairwell to check on Josephine. Rohan waited with her until more rescuers brought in equipment to help lift her out. It was nearly 6:00 P.M. when they finally dropped a contraption known as a Stokes basket down into the stairwell and brought up the grandmother from Brooklyn.

## MAYOR GIULIANI
**"He answered the same questions over and over."**

After staying in the Greenwich Village firehouse for a little over an hour, Mayor Giuliani moved his headquarters to the Police Academy on 20th Street. The first thing he did was call a meeting of all his aides and city commissioners. Everyone sat around a large table, and the mayor took notes as he went from one to the other and listened to their reports. Giuliani faced myriad decisions and logistical problems. What hospitals needed water or bandages? What trucks were available to deliver supplies? Where did one buy 18-gauge needles? Who could provide several thousand facemasks? How many bulldozers were there in the city at that moment? What could be done about restoring electricity downtown? Telephones? What construction sites around the city had cranes that could be brought downtown? How many city buses could be requisitioned for transportation duty?

After the meeting, the mayor held a formal news conference, the first of many he gave that day. Giuliani's top priority was to stay in touch with the people of New York, give them all the information he had, issue instructions, and try to calm fears. Televised news conferences seemed the best way to do it. Everybody in the city who wasn't fleeing downtown was probably in front of a television set.

Giuliani's day evolved into a routine of situation meetings, news conferences, and forays into the streets. He visited hospitals, talked personally to families of firefighters and police officers, and returned four times to Ground Zero to see the destruction firsthand, the last time shortly after midnight.

The day was also one of personal grief for Giuliani. Almost every hour, he learned about the death of a friend or colleague. He was told that both Chief Ganci and Father Judge had been killed, the priest as he gave last rites to a firefighter at Ground Zero. At Giuliani's first news conference, as he answered a question about the rescue effort, he suddenly thought of Terry Hatton, the husband of his executive assistant, Beth Petrone. Hatton was the captain of a fire department rescue unit. After the conference, he asked Beth if Terry had been on duty. She nodded yes, tears in her eyes, and he knew that Hatton was dead.

During his two terms as mayor, Giuliani had a sometimes contentious relationship with the news media, often chiding reporters for asking redundant questions. They, in turn, accused him of being imperious. At his news conferences on

September 11, Giuliani was always flanked by Governor George Pataki, Fire Commissioner Thomas Von Essen, and Police Commissioner Kerik. He frequently turned the microphone over to them to address specific questions, and he answered the same questions from reporters over and over in a calm, patient voice. If he didn't know something, he said, "I don't know the answer to that, but I'll try to find out and report back to you next time."

**Firefighters recovered the body of their chaplain, Father Mychal Judge, and carried him to a nearby church.**

The only issue the mayor refused to discuss that day was any question involving how many people might have been killed. He was polite, almost apologetic, but he would not be drawn into casualty estimates. "I don't think we yet know the pain we're going to feel when we find out who we lost," Giuliani replied when asked about the death toll. "In the end the number of casualties will be more than we can bear."

**Mayor Giuliani, Governor George Pataki, and Senator Hillary Rodham Clinton visited the ruins of the World Trade Center the day after the attacks.**

## MAC LAFOLLETTE
### "The streets were totally empty."

As they watched television, Mac LaFollette and Dawn Davis knew they had to do something. The one thing that immediately occurred to them was that they could donate blood for what were still expected to be thousands of wounded. Their houseguest, Andy, said he would join them.

It was shortly after noon when they got to St. Vincent's Hospital, between 11th and 12th Streets on Seventh Avenue, and there were already nearly 1,000 people waiting to give blood. The hospital was telling newcomers they could not take any more donations, and suggested they try at other hospitals. Mac, Dawn, and Andy walked around Greenwich Village for a while, when Mac suddenly had an idea. They were not far from the Salvation Army headquarters on 14th Street. Maybe they could find something to do there—make sandwiches, hand out food, anything. It was early afternoon when they arrived, and a truck loaded with bottles of water was about to head downtown toward Ground Zero. Mac and Andy jumped on the back. Dawn returned home.

The truck drove down West Street, but it was stopped about ten blocks north of the World Trade Center. From there,

Mac, Andy, and the others in the Salvation Army crew carried cases of water by hand from the truck to a spot just a couple of blocks north of the World Trade Center.

For the next two hours, Mac handed out bottles of water, mostly to firefighters, but also to police officers and emergency medical service personnel. The firefighters, who were now battling blazes that had been ignited in other buildings in the Trade Center complex, wandered up, dazed and confused. Many said they were searching for their buddies who were missing in the collapsed towers. They gratefully took bottles of water, chug-a-lugged them, and then headed back either to fight fires or search for their mates.

**Offices, shops, and businesses in the area surrounding the World Trade Center were converted into emergency treatment centers or morgues.**

Late in the afternoon, fire officials told the Salvation Army crew they would have to leave the area. There was an alert that the other buildings might collapse, and all adjacent streets were being closed. Mac noticed that there were no roadblocks along the West Side Highway, and there was nothing to prevent them from going farther south rather than turning around and going back uptown.

The Salvation Army driver headed farther downtown, toward Battery Park City, a landfill that was made from earth removed when the World Trade Center was built. It was now an oasis of tranquility at the southern tip of Manhattan, where mothers and nannies who lived in surrounding apartment buildings often took babies and children to play.

When Mac got out of the truck, he saw a cluster of baby carriages, maybe thirty or more, all bunched together and abandoned. He could imagine the scene, as mothers grabbed their infants and fled, leaving the carriages behind as first one then a second airplane crashed into the towers only a few blocks away.

Mac continued to hand out bottles of water until the supply ran out. The Salvation Army truck returned north, but Mac didn't want to leave. He wanted to keep working, doing anything. He knew the area because he used to jog in Battery

Park City. So he walked around the back streets behind the Trade Center until he came out on the other side. Several businesses in the area had been converted to emergency use. A Brooks Brothers clothing store had been turned into a makeshift morgue, a triage and first-aid center had been set up in the lobby of a building across from Liberty Plaza, and a local Burger King outlet had been converted into a sort of warehouse. It had everything a firefighter or rescue worker might need. Spare construction helmets, goggles, masks, and gloves were stored there, in addition to mounds of donated food and bottled water that were being brought in from restaurants all over the city.

Once again, Mac began handing out water. But he noticed that some rescuers had formed bucket brigades to help remove debris in an effort to find survivors. As night approached, Mac and Andy went home to join Dawn for dinner. But Mac knew he had to return to Ground Zero, and after eating, he and Andy made their way back downtown.

The streets were totally empty. As they walked down Greenwich Street, the ruins of the World Trade Center glowed in the distance from the arc lights that had been set up to help the rescue workers. During the day, hundreds of New Yorkers had gone downtown, volunteering to help in the

**A fast-food restaurant became a temporary police station where donated food and equipment were stored for rescue workers.**

rescue effort. The police had set up a holding area, where they could wait until they were needed. But Mac did not want to wait, so he once again followed his old jogging path until he reached the Burger King at Liberty Plaza.

Mac and Andy went in, took goggles to protect their eyes from air that was still choked with smoke and ash and a mist of ground glass, then got on line and started picking up pieces of steel and concrete and tossing them in the buckets.

There were several lines working. At the end of each line, the bucket was emptied into one of the scores of dumpsters that had been parked nearby. Then the bucket was handed back down the line to be filled again. Mac took turns on the line, sometimes passing buckets, sometimes emptying them in the dumpsters. It was slow, laborious, and inefficient. But it was all the rescuers could do at the time, and time was critical.

The scene that night was eerie and bizarre. One sight captured the full attention of all the workers on the bucket lines. Just across the street was the Deutsche Bank building, a medium-sized construction by skyscraper standards, but one

**Firefighters, police officers, and citizen volunteers formed bucket brigades to clear rubble from the site as they worked against time to find survivors.**

that still stood about forty stories tall. A gaping hole had been gouged in the side of the building, and sticking out of it was an enormous slab of concrete and steel. But the windows on the giant hunk jutting out of the side did not match those of the bank building itself. It was an enormous piece of the collapsed South Tower that had been hurled into the edifice like a javelin.

There was a general fear that the bank building could collapse at any moment. Several times during the night, someone would shout that the building was about to fall. Everyone would drop their buckets and run away. After a few minutes, they would all trickle back, pick up their buckets, and start removing rubble again.

The work was grueling and full of unknown dangers. The only light came from the floodlights trained on the main part of the wreckage to help those searching for survivors. It was not dark, but the ominous half-light made it difficult to see exactly where one was standing. Also, the bucket workers were not on firm ground but on small mounds of rubble from the collapsed towers. One wrong step and you could fall into a hole. Once Mac took a step back and looked behind him. There was a sheer drop of about twenty feet into a giant crater in the ground.

The bucket brigades worked in silence, almost afraid to talk lest they miss the squeak of a cellphone or some faint voice crying out from under the rubble. Occasionally, someone might say "hot" when a bucket filled with smoldering ruins was being passed along. Or there would suddenly be a shout of "Quiet!" Everyone would stop what they were doing, straining their ears to hear any sound that might be coming out of the rubble. A firefighter or police officer would usually hurry over with one of the sniffer dogs. Then, when no one was found, work would slowly resume.

Mac worked on past midnight, hoping he and the others on the bucket lines would find some trace of human life. They never found any.

. . . . . . . . . . . . . . . . . . . . . . . . .

## MY STORY
### "All the news was grim."

Work for me that day was simply going through the motions. It was shortly before 6:00 P.M. when I left for the day. During the time I had been at work, the city had become like a ghost town. Sixth Avenue was as empty at dusk as it had been packed at noon. I walked almost alone down the middle of the street.

Not a car was moving. Only a few other people were out.

By the time I reached Macy's, at 34th Street, I was staring at the downtown skyline. The towers weren't there, of course. In their place was this immense hole in the sky. In their place was nothing but fire and belching black, black smoke, still pouring out of the pile of rubble where the towers had been, a pile of rubble that itself was several stories tall. I couldn't watch for long. I looked away, at the shops that were closed and shuttered, at rush hour, or at the dozen or so other people who were, like me, walking in the middle of the street. Every block or so, I would look up again, hoping that when I did, the towers would be back, that this was just an illusion. But block after block, every time I would look up, they still weren't there. Just that same hole in the sky.

I was eager to get home so that I could catch up on what had happened during the hours I was at work. At the time, I was employed as an editor in the weekly *Book Review* at *The New York Times*. Although there were televisions on in the main newsroom, we were reluctant to go there just to satisfy our curiosity. Editors, reporters, and writers were trying to put out a newspaper, and we didn't want to interfere. Occasionally, coworkers came into the office to pass on stories or updates they had heard on television or radio, and my colleague David Kelly picked up some information from the Internet.

There was no good news that day. Life in America was pretty much grinding to a standstill. The stock markets stopped all trading and closed. Theaters canceled performances, and Broadway turned off its lights. Major League Baseball and the National Football League called off their games for the following week. In the afternoon we learned that buildings Number 4, 5, and 7 at the World Trade Center were all on fire—blazes set by the collapse of the North Tower—and there were fears those buildings might fall, too.

During the day, I talked once on the phone to LuAnn. Her meetings had been canceled and her office closed. She had walked downtown with some colleagues, and as soon as she arrived home, she went to buy bottled water in case the city's water supply was interrupted. She saw a long line stretching all the way down 12th Street from St. Vincent's Hospital, around the corner to the grocery store. At first she thought it was a line of people waiting to get into the supermarket to stock up on provisions. New Yorkers often have a tendency to buy a month's supply of food on the basis of a bad weather forecast. Then she realized that the line, more than two blocks long, was of people waiting to donate blood at the hospital.

From the time I walked into our apartment, LuAnn and I sat on the couch watching the story of that day replayed on television. No matter how many times we saw it, the film of the actual attacks on the Twin Towers still made us recoil, as though someone had hit us in the face. First there was the streak of the first plane plowing into the side of the North Tower. Then, just over a quarter of an hour later, there was the image of the second plane, dropping out of the sky in the west at a steep angle, flying at full speed, heading for the South Tower, crashing into it, and exploding in a fireball.

One of the most gripping stories that day had taken place within an hour of the attacks on the Twin Towers and the Pentagon. The story of United Airlines Flight 93, out of Newark and bound for San Francisco, was beginning to be pieced together from reports of surviving family members who had received cellphone calls from passengers aboard the plane after it had been hijacked. When they called home from aboard the plane, they did not know what had happened in New York and Washington.

Jeremy Glick, the father of a twelve-week-old girl, had changed his plans at the last minute to catch an earlier flight to San Francisco for a business meeting. About an hour after the flight took off, he called his wife, Lyzbeth, to tell her that three men wearing red headbands had taken over the plane. He said they had knives and that one of them said a red box he was holding contained a bomb. Lyzbeth, who had been watching the coverage of the attacks on the Twin Towers and Pentagon on television, agonized over whether to tell her husband about them. In the end, she knew she had to.

Thomas E. Burnett Jr. and Mark Bingham were two other passengers aboard United Flight 93 who made cellphone calls home. In each case, family members were torn over whether to pass on the information about what had already happened, but like Lyzbeth Glick, they did. Once Burnett and Bingham learned about the attacks in New York and at the Pentagon, they knew that they had to act to avert another catastrophe. If they were about to die, they were determined they would not let the hijackers crash the plane into some other heavily populated building or a national landmark like the Capitol or the White House.

Finally, Burnett told his wife that he and three or four other passengers were "getting ready to do something." He said one passenger had already been stabbed to death. Burnett's wife, Deena, the mother of three young daughters, pleaded with him not to upset the hijackers.

"No, no," he said. "If they're going to run this into the ground, we're going to have to do something." He hung up abruptly and never called back.

In his last call to his wife of five years, Glick told her not to be sad and to take care of their daughter. Bingham also made one final call to his parents and told them, "I just want you guys to know I love you very much."

United Flight 93 crashed in a rural field near Shanksville, Pennsylvania, at 10:10 A.M.

The reports that night of the attack on the Pentagon were also chilling. American Airlines Flight 77 crashed into the western side of the five-storied, five-sided building that housed the nation's military headquarters. The explosion and ensuing fire caused a part of the wall to collapse inward, killing more than 120 people.

**United Flight 93 crashed into a field in Pennsylvania after some passengers, told what had happened in New York, decided to overpower its hijackers.**

In a separate attack, another hijacked plane, American Airlines Flight 77, was flown into the side of the Pentagon, in Washington, D.C.

The plane flew into a part of the Pentagon that had recently been renovated with new safety equipment, such as shatterproof windows, and officials said the death toll could have been higher without them.

There had also been cellphone calls from that plane before it flew into the Pentagon. One of the fifty-eight passengers on Flight 77 was Barbara Olson, a television political commentator and the wife of Theodore Olson, the solicitor general of the United States. In the first call, Mrs. Olson told her husband that the plane was being hijacked, but that call abruptly ended. A few moments later, she called back to say that the pilot and crew of the plane had been herded to the rear of the aircraft, and that the hijackers had taken over the cockpit. She asked her husband if there was anything she should tell the pilot to do.

Theodore Olson did not have any advice for the pilot. Like Lyzbeth Glick, he too had been following the news of the World Trade Center attacks on television. He knew what to expect, and he told his wife what had happened in New York. They said their final farewells and Mrs. Olson hung up.

After being alerted by air controllers about the first hijackings, air force jets had scrambled into the sky to try to intercept American Flight 77. But by the time they reached the Pentagon, the plane had already crashed into it. Fires burned through the day at the building, but by nightfall they had been brought under control.

All the news that night was grim. The numbers alone were almost unbelievable. When Mayor Giuliani said at a news conference that more than 250 firefighters had been "lost," I thought for a split second he meant just that—they were lost, they hadn't reported in to their battalion chiefs, something like that. The figure was just too monumental. In the end, it was a conservative estimate. In the end, 343 firefighters died.

Mayor Giuliani still declined to give any estimate on the number of people who may have died. But when he said that at least 20,000 people had been working in the buildings at the time of the attacks, it was clear that thousands of people had been killed. It was a shock, although LuAnn and I both had known that the figures would be high. After all, it had been reported that the first call to a hospital that morning, minutes after the attacks, had not been for ambulances or doctors, but for body bags.

We listened in silence to reports on the other buildings that had been damaged. Building Number 7 had collapsed, and three other structures in the Trade Center complex were in danger of falling. A hotel was destroyed, as was a footbridge that led to the World Financial Center. Apartment buildings in the blocks surrounding the Trade Center were deemed unsafe or unhealthful and had been evacuated. Thousands of people who lived in Battery Park City were told they could not enter the buildings, even to rescue their pets.

As we watched past midnight, the reports from television anchors were underscored by live shots from Ground Zero. Throughout the night, firefighters, police officers, emergency workers, and civilian volunteers clawed through the ruins, looking for survivors. The rescuers had brought kennels of dogs to the site to try to sniff out life—or death—in the mountain of rubble. But there were so many torn bodies, the dogs would get confused and rush from one pile of smoldering debris to another.

The agony and frustration visible on the faces of the fire-fighters, police officers, and rescue workers were heartbreaking. The chance of anyone being found alive under the tons of steel and cement was microscopic at best. Yet on and on they worked, hour after hour.

The sense of helplessness was reflected in one story of an emergency medical station that was set up along the Hudson to treat the large numbers of wounded that were expected to overflow from the hospitals. The doctors had set out dozens of cots, unrolled bandages, kept pints of blood ready, and even prepared little colored tabs to triage the injured survivors they expected to start arriving in ambulances at any moment. Then they waited. And waited. And waited. One hour, two hours, three hours. Not a single injured person was brought in. At first they were puzzled. Then they began to understand. There were no survivors for the ambulances to rescue.

# THE AFTERMATH

## JIM KENWORTHY
**"The apartment became a constant reminder."**

In the days immediately following the attack, Jim Kenworthy was never far from the telephone. He kept all calls to a minimum in case the miracle call came from a hospital, saying that Ginger was there. He knew how long the odds were, but when the only thread of hope is a telephone line, you keep it open.

Jim listened closely to news reports on the progress of the search for survivors. Every time there was a report of someone being found alive, his hopes would rise. There were several such stories in the days immediately following the attacks. One said that five people had been found alive in a car in the garage of the Twin Towers. Another report said that someone had survived the actual collapse, had ridden the building down, and suffered only two broken legs. Jim heard yet another that someone from a floor above Ginger's had gotten out alive. All turned out to be false. No one was found alive after the first day. The miracle phone call never came.

Beth and Billie had a difficult time. Each was depressed, and Billie sometimes would burst into uncontrollable crying, especially at night. Jim would wake up in the night and hear him sobbing in his room. Both children had a thousand questions, but they all pretty much boiled down to one. Why? And, of course, there was no answer to that.

Slowly Jim, Beth, and Billie tried to return to some sort of routine. Beth and Billie both decided they wanted to resume their piano lessons, and they began playing soccer again. But Beth, who had been a standout on both the girls' and boys' teams, did not play as well now. Teammates would kick her the ball, and she would run down the field. But she was easily distracted and found it hard to focus on the game. She did not have the same aggressive edge that she had when both Jim and Ginger were there cheering her on. Nothing interested her, and she would go out of her way to avoid any kind of confrontation.

Billie, who had always been the more easygoing and accepting of the two, now felt defensive about every little thing that anybody said or did. He got into fights, something he had not done before. It happened twice at school. He was never sure whether he would burst into tears or strike out at something. Neither of the children's grades changed noticeably at school, but they were not happy.

Jim kept a close watch on the children. He consulted a doctor and learned the warning signs to look for in their behavior in case they might need outside help or counseling. He also had to battle his own imponderables. A photo of the family taken at the beach on Long Island just weeks before the attack brought aching regrets that the life they had together was now lost. He consoled himself with the thought that he and Ginger had improved their lives during the time they had together. Still, Jim had to work daily on not speculating about the "what ifs" of that horrible day. He knew for certain, however, that if he had gone downtown and tried to be heroic, he and Ginger would both be dead.

The apartment that Jim and Ginger had put so much work into became a constant reminder of her. If Jim went for a glass of water, he was reminded of how they had saved to install a brand-new kitchen, and of all the evenings he cooked pasta while Ginger entertained their friends at the dining table. If he opened one of the closets and saw a pair of skis, he would think of their honeymoon in Switzerland and the ski vacations they took almost every winter. Ginger had loved to ski and he had had to learn. If his eyes fell on the piano, he remembered how Ginger had gotten both Beth and Billie interested in music. If he saw a soccer ball in the corner, he thought about how the sport had become such a big part of their lives. Everywhere Jim Kenworthy looked in the apartment, he saw Ginger.

Finally, when all hope was gone, and at the urging of Ginger's mother, Jim arranged a memorial service for his wife at New York's First Presbyterian Church. Ginger and he had joined the church after they married, and Ginger had been active in it. The service was conducted by the Reverend Barrie Shepherd, a pastor emeritus at the church, with whom Ginger had been close. In his homily, Dr. Shepherd cited the Apostles' Creed, and the passage in which some Christians affirm their belief that Jesus "descended into Hell." Dr. Shepherd noted that some denominations omit the reference to hell. "Then came September 11," he said, "and we saw hell. Right down the street here, not many blocks away, we glimpsed not only evil; we saw hell."

It was an emotional service, and Billie wept like rain all the way through it. But in the days afterward, he stopped crying at night.

**BOB FOX**
*"Those firefighters had saved his life."*

Bob Fox could not watch or read any of the coverage of the attacks for days. If the television was on and the subject of the attack on the Twin Towers came up, he would go into another room. He selectively scanned the newspapers, avoiding most articles about the attacks. He talked to Ray Miller and learned with relief that their other three colleagues who had been in the office that morning—Nick Pipinic, Bob Cristobel, and Nadine Vesio—had all made it out alive. Ray told him that after he and Bob had become separated, Ray had been knocked down by the rush of wind when the tower collapsed.

And Bob learned the one thing that he had been most fearful to discover. Tim O'Sullivan's body had been found on the main lobby level of the ruins of the World Trade Center, along with those of the two firefighters who had taken charge of Tim and had ordered Bob and Ray to evacuate the building. The firefighters had, in fact, gotten Tim down. But too late.

Bob tried to keep busy with work. He knew that it was vital for the Cultural Institutions Retirement System to get back on its feet as soon as possible. All of the System's records had been lost in the collapse of the North Tower, but

Firefighter Patrick Parrott lights a candle at one of the memorials that sprang up at firehouses throughout New York. This one honors the fourteen firefighters from Engine 54, Ladder 4, who died in the collapse of the Twin Towers.

duplicates were stored in a bank in Boston. The day after the attack, Bob set about finding temporary office space, and within a week he had found a place in New Jersey. But he was also determined to find a new headquarters back in New York City.

Bob found himself thinking a lot about the two firefighters who tried to help Tim, and of Captain Mazza, the Port Authority officer who gave Tim oxygen. Although neither he nor Ray nor Tim had known what had happened to the South Tower, the firefighters probably did. They knew that the North Tower could collapse at any minute. Yet they stayed behind, helping as many civilians reach safety as they could. Bob knew that those firefighters had saved his life. He knew they had died doing so.

Although he attended several memorial services after the attack, Bob felt personally indebted to two men whose names he did not even know, and he had no idea how to acknowledge his gratitude. Finally, he wrote an open letter to "All Members of the New York City Fire Department and Their Families" that both he and Ray signed.

In it, he recalled his and Ray's particular experience and said in conclusion: "We want to say thank you to all the firefighters. . . . [We] share in your loss."

## OMAR RIVERA
### "He heard airplanes everywhere."

At the time he had gone blind, Omar Rivera learned that the best way to combat depression was to stay busy. Do anything, but keep active. But the days following the attack found Omar at home with little to do. With so much time on his hands, he relived the horrors of that day over and over. Without a job to go to, Omar would wander about his house, going from room to room, with Salty following along beside him.

Sounds, on which he had learned to rely as signposts, began to terrify him. He heard airplanes everywhere, the drone of their engines haunting him.

Omar had trouble sleeping. He would lie in bed awake, the sounds of people screaming or praying on the stairs of the North Tower, of steel girders snapping, echoing in his head. One night several days after the attack, as sleep was finally about to reach him, an alarm sounded from a fire station near his house. He shot up in bed, woke Sonia and their three daughters, got them all together, and had them all kneel and pray.

Music had always been a big part of Omar's life, especially after his blindness, and after September 11, he found himself listening to certain pieces of music over and over. His favorite music was classical guitar, but he also had a collection of Colombian folk music that he liked because the songs tell stories. One is about a traveler who has lost his way. The chorus goes: "There is no path, there is no road. You have to make your own path." Omar played it constantly.

The Port Authority set up temporary offices in New Jersey, and Omar returned to work. It was an even more arduous commute —from New Rochelle to Grand Central, then a New York City subway to a PATH train to New Jersey—and took man and dog about two and a half hours each way.

But the routine was good for Omar and Salty. It got them out of the house and gave structure to their days. Salty calmed down, although at the sound of any siren or alarm, the dog went to get his harness so that he and Omar could leave.

. . . . . . . . . .

## LADDER COMPANY 6
### "Josephine Harris went home to Brooklyn."

After emerging from the ruins of the North Tower, the firefighters of Ladder 6 went separate ways. Meldrum, who had a concussion, and Komorowski, who had a separated shoulder, were taken to a hospital. Picciotto also was taken to an emer-

Josephine Harris visited the firefighters of Ladder Company 6, who turned out in dress uniform to welcome their "guardian angel." Pictured, from left, are: Matt Komorowski, Tommy Falco, Sal D'Agostino, Josephine Harris, Captain Jonas, Bill Butler, and Mike Meldrum.

gency ward, suffering from burns and cuts to his eyes. Falco and Butler were sent home.

Captain Jonas decided he should get back to his firehouse. A police officer gave him a ride to Canal Street, and from there, he walked across Manhattan to Ladder 6 headquarters. All along the way, as he made his way through Chinatown, people on the sidewalks cheered and applauded him. Jonas was later promoted to battalion chief.

Josephine Harris went home to Brooklyn. Her grandchildren were ecstatic to see her. Throughout the day they had not known whether she was alive or dead.

A couple of weeks later, she visited the firehouse in Chinatown. All of the firefighters gave her a hero's reception and had their picture taken with her in their dress uniforms. For the firefighters of Ladder 6, Josephine was their guardian angel. If they had not stopped to take care of her, and had rushed to get out of the building, they probably would have been killed on the lower floors.

· · · · · · · · · · · · · · · · · · · · · · · · · · · · · ·

## MAYOR GIULIANI
### "He grabbed New York City by its lapels."

On the night of the attacks, when Mayor Giuliani finally went home shortly before 1:00 A.M., he got into bed and read a new biography about Winston Churchill, Britain's prime minister during World War II, who led the country through three months of almost nonstop bombing attacks on London by the Nazis. He told friends he learned something that night, and over the next days and weeks the mayor urged, cajoled, and challenged New Yorkers to carry on with their daily lives, the way Londoners had done during the Blitz. By word and example, Rudy Giuliani almost single-handedly grabbed New York City by its lapels and dragged it back to its feet.

**Funerals for fallen comrades were held in the days following the attack. Carl Vasquez, Jay Robbins, and Dennis McLane, all emergency medical technicians, salute in memory of Yemel Marino, who died at the World Trade Center.**

In the days that followed, Giuliani was the last person one saw before turning off the television at night and the first person one saw on television in the morning. He seemed to be everywhere. He was at Ground Zero, at hospitals, at firehouses, at news conferences, at private homes. There were days the mayor attended as many as eight funerals or memorial services. He broke down and wept at a ceremony in which 168 firefighters were promoted to higher ranks to fill vacancies left by those who had been killed.

Giuliani spoke at a memorial service in St. Patrick's Cathedral for victims at Marsh & McLennan, the company for which Ginger Ormiston had worked. In his address the mayor told the families of those killed: "We have to cry. But the tears have to make us stronger. We are bound together and we're going to remain bound together."

. . . . . . . . . . . . . . . . . . . . . .

## MAC LAFOLLETTE
### "The work was simple, slow digging."

Mac LaFollette spent the day after the attack at home with his wife, Dawn, and his friend Andy, watching the television coverage of the attacks. At one point, they went out for a walk. On street corners and in parks, there were already small memorials being erected for those killed in the attacks — candles with photographs and small mementos. Silent knots of people stood on the street, staring downtown at the smoke still rising above the empty skyline.

On the following day, Mac and Andy decided to return to Ground Zero and volunteer again for the rescue work. When they reached downtown, they encountered scenes of

As hope for finding survivors faded, city construction workers and a professional demolition company joined the cleanup operation while still searching for the remains of victims. Someone raised a flag over the ruins of the World Trade Center.

**Rescue workers, both humans and dogs,
slept when and where they could.**

devastation that were worse than anything Mac had seen in the
third-world countries he had visited. Wrecked and charred cars
were piled up four or five deep, one on top of the other. Stores
and shops were burned out and demolished.

This time, everything at Ground Zero was more organized. There were now metalworkers with blowtorches to cut up the larger pieces of steel, and cranes were being brought in to lift some of the beams. But the brunt of the work was still simple, slow digging, and there were hundreds of New Yorkers wanting to join the search for survivors. Some brought their own shovels. Volunteers were directed to a waiting area until they were assigned to a team of workers. Mac again ended up on a bucket brigade.

The work was tedious and painstaking and dangerous. Fires still burned and the debris was often hot to touch. Mac knew they had no hope now of finding people alive. They were sifting through tons of rubble from two 110-story office buildings, and they had not found any desks, chairs, computers, or even telephones intact. Everything except the steel beams had been pulverized. What chance would a human being have had?

In the nights that followed, Mac began to have a nightmare. In it, he was working the bucket brigades, and everyone was passing him pieces of metal that were twisted like pretzels, and it was his job to sort them all out and rebuild the Twin Towers.

## MY STORY
**"Each flier told a heartbreaking story."**

For LuAnn and myself, like the rest of New York, there was no escaping September 11. Turning off the television did not help. Walking to the grocery store or the cleaners, we would see reminders everywhere of how many people had died. Within hours of the collapse of the Twin Towers, fliers with pictures and telephone numbers of people who were missing began appearing. The fliers often contained information about the person, and by September 12 there were thousands of them everywhere—store windows, street lamps, the sides of buildings. As I left home to walk to work or pick up milk at the store, I would stop and read some of them. Each told a heartbreaking story.

A residue of fear covered the city like the clouds of acrid smoke and ash that still hung in the air. No one believed that the attacks on the Twin Towers and Pentagon were isolated strikes. There might be another attack any day. Some terrorist groups were believed to be working on small nuclear weapons and experimenting with biological and chemical weapons. Would the next attack be with smallpox, the plague, anthrax, or some other deadly disease? Or would it be on a nuclear power plant?

Mayor Giuliani was constantly urging New Yorkers to continue with their daily lives or else the terrorists would have won an even greater victory. LuAnn and I went to work, although it was hard to find much enthusiasm in our jobs. In the days and weeks that followed, we went to Yankee Stadium, ate out in restaurants, went to the opera, a museum, and the theater. We were not looking for diversion. It was the only way we knew to fight back.

(718) 375-9777
(917) 370-1708

Warning
White Shirt
Blue Jeans
Eyeglasses

JUAN GARCIA
(917) 492-2474

GERARD RAUZI

WTCMISSING.ORG

CHET LOUIE
12-1-57
PLEASE CALL:

If you have any information

MISSING PERSON
MARGARET ECHTERMANN

MISSING
NYC FIREM
PAUL KEAT
CONTACT # 1-732-9

MISSING
Cantor Fitzgerald employee 104th Floor
Richard Caggiano
Jude Safi
Robert Tipaldi
Contact: (718) 549-4334
(718) 825-5586
(718) 493-2443

CALL 212-923-0419

CALL 617-241-5091

MISSING

PLEASE HELP US FIND

Ralph Licciardi

Aida Rosario Vazquez

GILLEEN SUPINSKI AGE 27

MISSING
David Pruim

Missing at the WTC 2

# EPILOGUE

New York and the rest of the country returned to life slowly. By the weekend, planes were flying. On Monday, Wall Street resumed trading, and America reopened for business. After a week, the Major Leagues and the National Football League resumed their schedule of games. The curtains went up on Broadway. Stores and restaurants reopened. But for many, the nightmare of September 11 was replayed over and over. For many, it became a day that will never end.

New York City went into a sort of perpetual mourning over the next few weeks. The sounds of drums, pipes, and bugles echoed across the city as dirges were played at hundreds of funerals and memorial services. Mayor Giuliani became the city's chief eulogist.

After the initial shock of September 11, the question of exactly who had carried out the attack began to grow. The FBI

**Hundreds of memorial sevices for firefighters and
police officers were held throughout New York.**

identified nineteen of the passengers aboard the four jets as the
hijackers, and Mohamed Atta as the ringleader. But somebody,
somewhere, had planned, financed, and executed the attacks
on the World Trade Center and Pentagon. One name kept
coming up: Osama bin Laden, the wealthy son of a Saudi
Arabian businessman, who ran the militant Islamic organization
known as Al Qaeda and operated terrorist training camps in
Afghanistan. As the investigation traced the background of
the hijackers, the common thread was a connection with
Al Qaeda.

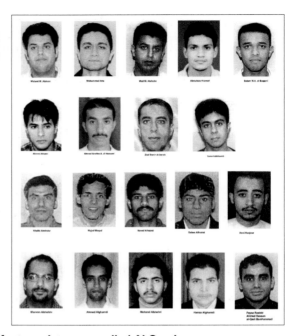

**Osama bin Laden, leader of a terrorist group called Al Qaeda, authorized the attacks, which were carried out by nineteen men, some of whom did not know they were on suicide missions.**

The investigation also discovered that some of the hijackers probably did not know they were going to die. A long handwritten letter found in Atta's luggage, which had not made the connection on his flight from Maine to Boston, made clear that he was leading a suicide attack. But investigators also found letters that Atta had written to other hijackers in which he had urged them to be strong in prison. Some hijackers thought that at worst they would wind up in jail.

The United States sent emissaries to its traditional allies in Europe and to countries in the Middle East to provide details of its case that Al Qaeda, and by complicity the ruling Taliban regime in Afghanistan, had been behind the attacks. Meanwhile, military commanders at the damaged Pentagon were planning to strike back.

On October 7, 2001, American and British warplanes launched an attack on Afghanistan. The air strikes were aimed at bringing down the Taliban regime, which had protected and supported Al Qaeda. Within weeks, the Taliban was overthrown, and its leaders, along with bin Laden and his Al Qaeda cohorts, had fled to the desolate mountains along the Afghanistan border with Pakistan. But no one had any illusions that removing the Taliban from power in Afghanistan would somehow end the terrorist threat. The United States, working with intelligence and police departments around the world, quietly began a long and methodical search for anyone, anywhere, with a link to Al Qaeda.

The work at Ground Zero focused on recovering the bodies of as many victims as possible that might be buried under the more than 3 billion pounds of steel and concrete. The New York Fire Department was in charge, and up to 100 firefighters were on duty there around the clock. A construction company, Bovis Lend Lease, was hired to clear the site, and the bucket brigades were replaced by bulldozers and cranes. Firefighters and construction workers sifted through the debris, looking for any remains of those who had been killed. Each time part of a victim was found, it was taken to the offices of Dr. Charles S. Hirsch, the chief medical examiner for New York City, where teams of pathologists, dentists, fingerprint experts, and DNA specialists worked nonstop in sixteen refrigerated trailers parked nearby to try to put names to the remains so that the families of those who died could hold funerals for them.

On May 30, 2002, the last steel girder of the World Trade Center was hauled off. On June 25, nine months and two weeks after the attacks, the fire department formally ended the recovery operation. The site where the Twin Towers had stood had been leveled, and the area around it had been swept. With little fanfare, the last four firefighters left. A city construction worker sang the Irish ballad "Danny Boy," and the firefighters draped a flag over the steel box that contained the last possible remains to be taken from Ground Zero.

On the first anniversary of the attacks, memorial services were held at the Pentagon, in the open field in Pennsylvania, and at the World Trade Center. As part of the commemoration at Ground Zero, the names of 2,801 victims of the three attacks were read aloud. It took nearly three hours to read the names of all the people who died.

On May 30, 2002, families of victims joined police officers and firefighters in a ceremony as the last steel girder of the World Trade Center was hauled away from Ground Zero. A stretcher with an American flag covering it symbolized all those who died and whose bodies were never recovered.

## ▪ Acknowledgments ▪

I wish this book had never been written. That is to say, I wish there had never been a reason for it to be written. After the events of September 11, 2001, I knew that any account of that day could come only from the people who lived through it. It is with an immense debt of gratitude that I recognize the fortitude of three people who agreed to relive the horrors of that day and revisit the agony and pain they endured: James Kenworthy, Omar Rivera, and Robert Fox. This is their book.

I also want to thank Mac LaFollette for sharing his experiences of that day and night. It would be remiss of me not to acknowledge the many journalists who covered the events of September 11 and whose accounts provided information about the firefighters of Ladder Company 6, Mayor Rudolph Giuliani, the attack on the Pentagon, and the crash in Pennsylvania. Among those who contributed to the book in special ways are the Rev. Barrie Shepherd, pastor emeritus of the First Presbyterian Church of New York; Bill Badger, owner of Guiding Eyes for the Blind; and Dr. Alan J. Friedman, director of the New York Hall of Science.

It is to Amy Ehrlich, my editor, that I owe the opportunity to undertake this project. Her faith in the book sustained me when my own faltered, her focus clarified it when my own blurred, and her patience calmed me when my own wore thin. Every writer should have such an editor. Many others at Candlewick Press contributed at different steps along the way, especially Cynthia Platt and Cecile Proverbs with their valuable editorial advice, and Sherry Fatla with her design.

And finally, as always, I am indebted to the abiding inspiration of my wife, LuAnn Walther.

## ▪ Bibliography ▪

Giuliani, Rudolph W. *The Quotable Giuliani: The Mayor of America in His Own Words*. Edited by Bill Adler Jr. New York: Pocket Books, 2002.

Hersey, John. *Hiroshima*. New York: Vintage Books Edition, 1989.

Picciotto, Richard, with Daniel Paisner. *Last Man Down: A New York City Fire Chief and the Collapse of the World Trade Center*. New York: Berkley Books, 2002.

Smith, Dennis. *Report from Ground Zero: The Story of the Rescue Efforts at the World Trade Center*. New York: Viking Press, 2002.

## ▪ Filmography ▪

*In Memoriam: New York City*. HBO, 2002.

Naudet, Jules and Gédéon. *9/11: The Filmmakers' Commemorative Edition*. CBS, 2002.

# ▪ Index ▪

## ▪ Photo Credits ▪

## Uncaptioned Photographs

**Wilborn Hampton** is the author of *Kennedy Assassinated! The World Mourns: A Reporter's Story; Meltdown: A Race Against Nuclear Disaster at Three Mile Island;* and *War in the Middle East: A Reporter's Story: Black September and the Yom Kippur War.* He works at *The New York Times,* previously as a theater and book critic, and most recently as an editor on the foreign news desk.

Although he did not cover the attacks of September 11, 2001, he undertook to write the story of that awful day because he felt that "no single event since the attack on Pearl Harbor has so traumatized and galvanized the American people. It seemed important, especially for younger readers who may have questions about what happened in years to come, to try to put on paper an account of what took place in New York City that day. And the only way to begin to understand the horror of what occurred on September 11 was to recount it through the eyes of those who experienced it firsthand."